# Text and Story

# Text and Story
*Narrative Studies in New Testament Textual Criticism*

Peter R. Rodgers

☙PICKWICK *Publications* • Eugene, Oregon

TEXT AND STORY
Narrative Studies in New Testament Textual Criticism

Copyright © 2011 Peter R. Rodgers. All rights reserved. Except for brief quotations in critical publications or reviews, no part of this book may be reproduced in any manner without prior written permission from the publisher. Write: Permissions, Wipf and Stock Publishers, 199 W. 8th Ave., Suite 3, Eugene, OR 97401.

Pickwick Publications
An Imprint of Wipf and Stock Publishers
199 W. 8th Ave., Suite 3
Eugene, OR 97401

www.wipfandstock.com

ISBN 13: 978-1-61097-304-5

*Cataloging-in-Publication data:*

Rodgers, Peter R.

   Text and story : narrative studies in New Testament textual criticism / Peter R. Rodgers.

      x + 126 p. ; 23 cm. Including bibliographical references and indexes.

      ISBN 13: 978-1-61097-304-5

      1. Bible. N.T.—Criticism, Textual. 2. Bible. N.T.—Criticism, Narrative. I. Title.

BS2325 R55 2011

Manufactured in the U.S.A.

*For Kathy, Mark, Ben, and Amanda*

# Contents

*Abbreviations* • ix

Introduction • 1

1. Romans 8:28 • 17
2. Luke 3:22 • 22
3. Hebrews 2:9 • 31
4. Mark 15:34 • 44
5. Luke 22:43–44 • 54
6. Acts 20:28 • 62
7. Philippians 4:7 • 72
8. Romans 8:2 • 77
9. Mark 9:29 • 84
10. Luke 4:18 • 93

*Conclusion* • 101

*Appendix* • 107

*Bibliography* • 109

*Index of Names* • 117

*Index of Scripture and Ancient Sources* • 121

# Abbreviations

| | |
|---|---|
| *AB* | *Anchor Bible* |
| *ABD* | *Anchor Bible Dictionary* |
| ANF | Ante-Nicene Fathers |
| BCE | Before the Common Era |
| BECNT | Baker Exegetical Commentary on the New Testament |
| *BJRL* | *Bulletin of the John Rylands Library* |
| *CBQ* | *Catholic Biblical Quarterly* |
| CE | Common Era |
| *CJT* | *Canadian Journal of Theology* |
| *DTIB* | *Dictionary for Theological Interpretation of the Bible* |
| ICC | International Critical Commentary |
| *JBL* | *Journal of Biblical Literature* |
| *JTS* | *Journal of Theological Studies* |
| KJV | King James Bible |
| LNTS | Library of New Testament Studies |
| LXX | Septuagint |
| MM | Moulton and Milligan, *Vocabulary* |
| MT | Masoretic Text |
| NA$^{26}$ | Nestle–Aland, *Novum Testamentum Graece*, 26th edition |
| NA$^{27}$ | Nestle–Aland, *Novum Testamentum Graece*, 27th edition |
| NEB | New English Bible |
| *NETS* | *New English Translation of the Septuagint* |
| NIGTC | New International Greek Testament Commentary |
| NIV | New International Version |
| *NovT* | *Novum Testamentum* |
| NRSV | New Revised Standard Version |

| | | |
|---|---|---|
| NTS | *New Testament Studies* | |
| RBL | *Review of Biblical Literature* | |
| REB | Revised English Bible | |
| *RivB* | *Revista biblica italiana* | |
| RSR | *Recherches de science religieuse* | |
| RSV | Revised Standard Version | |
| TDNT | *Theological Dictionary of the New Testament* | |
| UBS[1][2][3][4] | United Bible Societies Greek New Testament (four editions) | |
| WBC | Word Biblical Commentary | |
| WH | Westcott and Hort, *The New Testament in the Original Greek* | |

# Introduction

The purpose of this book is to make a subject students often consider boring and complicated into one that is exciting and accessible. The subject is New Testament textual criticism. Textual criticism is both a science and an art. It is the science of discovering how and why a text has been corrupted in the course of copying, and the art of restoring it to its original form.[1] The textual criticism of the New Testament begins with the scientific study of a vast amount of data, which includes over 5,800 Greek manuscripts, translations into Latin, Syriac, Coptic, and a host of other languages, and quotations in early Christian writers. This data comprises the external material relating to the study of the text, and has been classified by scholars according to date, quality, affinity with other manuscripts, and text-type. Having analyzed and organized this data, the textual critic then seeks by the application of a number of principles, to determine which reading was most likely to have been written by the author. Among the factors considered are the "oldest and best manuscripts," the reading with the broadest geographical spread among the manuscripts, and the reading that best explains the rise of the alternative readings. In addition to the external data, there are other factors to consider. "Transcriptional probabilities" is a term used to describe the habits or choices of scribes as they copied manuscripts. Internal factors such as the style and theological perspective of the book in which the variation occurs need to be carefully considered in solving textual puzzles. In these latter considerations it will be clear that the practice of New Testament Textual Criticism requires not only the expertise of a scientist, but the talent of an artist.

In some cases the textual critic will have no difficulty in deciding on the original text (sometimes referred to as the "initial text"). Both external data (the manuscript evidence) and internal considerations (language and style, etc.) will tell in favor of one reading or another. For

---

1. Housman, "Application of Thought," 235.

example, in the case of the story of the woman taken in adultery (John 7:53—8:11) both factors indicate that the story was not original with John, but was added later by a scribe. Not only is the manuscript evidence for omitting it both early and diverse, but also the vocabulary and style are very different from the rest of the Gospel of John. Reviewing the evidence, Bruce Metzger wrote, "The case against its being of Johannine authorship appears to be conclusive."[2] But there are other points where the decision on the original reading is not as straightforward. For example, did Paul write "mystery" (μυστήριον) or "testimony" (μαρτύριον) in 1 Cor 2:1? The words in Greek are similar enough when either read or heard that the mistake might easily have arisen accidentally. For the textual critic the decision is not easy. In discussing this passage Gordon Fee puts the issue succinctly, "Did Paul write μυστήριον in anticipation of the argument in vv. 6–16, or did he write μαρτύριον, referring to his preaching in bearing witness to what God had done in Christ crucified?"[3] There are other places where the text critic finds that the external evidence (manuscripts) supports one reading and the internal considerations (style, theology) suggest another. Romans 5:1 is such an instance. Here the earliest manuscripts read "let us have peace," but the context clearly calls for the indicative, "we have peace." The difference in readings is between a long o (omega) and a short o (omicron). There are a number of places where the editors of the United Bible Societies Greek New Testament have chosen the reading with inferior manuscript support because of such internal considerations.[4] Such decisions on variant readings are not easy, and require that those who practice the discipline are both scientists and artists.

Decisions on textual questions can benefit from the discovery of new evidence, or from the refinement of methods within the discipline. The discovery of the papyri has greatly aided the study of the text in the past century. Some readings, formerly suspected to be original, now have a stronger claim because of these discoveries. For example, the reading "only-begotten God," in John 1:18 was carefully studied by F. J. A. Hort in 1876,[5] and Hort argued that this reading was original,

2. Metzger, *Textual Commentary*, 188.

3. Fee, "Textual-Exegetical Observations," 6.

4. See my tabulation for UBS³ in Peter R. Rodgers, "The New Eclecticism," 391 (reproduced as appendix). The text of UBS³/Nestle²⁶ is identical to that of UBS⁴/Nestle²⁷, see Nestle²⁷, 46* "The text of this edition reproduces the 26th edition unchanged."

5. Hort, *Two Dissertations*, 1–72.

rather than the words of the Authorized Version (KJV) "only-begotten Son." Now two important early papyri of the Gospel of John, P[66] and P[75], both discovered in the twentieth century, have notably strengthened the external support for "only-begotten God" (μονογενὴς θεὸς)[6] on this still much debated textual *crux interpretum*.

The textual critic has also been helped by the refinement of methods and criteria for evaluating variant readings. For example, one of the rules followed by modern textual critics of the New Testament is that the shorter reading is to be preferred (*lectio brevior potior*). However, some studies have raised questions about the value of this rule. E. C. Colwell, James R. Royce, and Peter M. Head studied scribal habits in the early papyri and found that the scribes of these earliest manuscripts were more prone to omit words from their texts than to add to them.[7] In assessing the evidence of the earliest manuscripts, other things being equal, the longer reading is to be preferred.

Another study conducted by Michael Holmes has further refined the evaluation of variations in the New Testament text. The assumption has been that scribes tended to harmonize a passage they were copying either to its parallel in another gospel or to a passage in the Old Testament where it was quoted by a New Testament writer. Holmes studied the passages in Matthew relating to divorce and re-marriage, and concluded that there was far less of a tendency to harmonize than is commonly assumed.[8] Careful studies in methodology combine with continual discovery of new evidence to aid the textual critic in the task of recovering the original text of the New Testament.

This book is intended to make a further contribution to the study of the text of the New Testament. My goal is to relate the field of New Testament Textual Criticism to the Narrative critical study of the New Testament. Hence the title of this study, *Text and Story*. This study is an experiment in the engagement of Narrative Criticism with Textual Criticism in the study of the New Testament. To date not much attention has been given to such an experiment. Indeed, there has been neglect on both fronts. I quote an example from one of the early and important studies in the Narrative Criticism of the New Testament. In *Mark as*

---

6. Metzger, *Textual Commentary*, 169–70.

7. See James R. Royce, *Scribal Habits*; E. C. Colwell, *Studies in Methodology*; and Peter M. Head, "Observations," 240–47.

8. Holmes, "The Text of the Matthean Divorce Passages," 651–64.

*Story*, David Rhoads and Donald Mitchie write, "We have not made reference to many important textual variations. For example, throughout our study we assume that Mark's gospel ends at 16:8."[9] Such an assumption not only begs the textual questions regarding the endings of Mark, but also fails to ask whether the study of Mark as story might have anything new to add to the textual question. In his recent study *Narrative Criticism of the New Testament,* James L. Resseguie makes only two references to Bruce Metzger's *Textual Commentary,* and in both cases the variations are merely mentioned and not discussed. In the first instance, Mark 1:1, the textual decision is of fundamental importance for interpreting the narrative shape of Mark.[10] Whether or not Mark wrote "the Son of God" in 1:1 dramatically impacts the way the reader responds to Mark's story. So there is a need for the study of text and story.

One problem we face in such a study is that "narrative" is a protean and multivalent term, especially when applied to biblical studies. In the study of the New Testament there have been at least two main senses in which the term is employed. Some have used the term *narrative criticism* to describe how biblical literature works as *literature.* This analysis looks at various elements of a written work: rhetoric, setting, character, point of view and plot. This study of the formal features in its finished form is similar to the kind of examination of any work of literature. Its aim is to discern how the readers, both original and subsequent, would have understood and responded to the text. This has become a very popular method of approach to New Testament documents in recent years.[11]

Another sense in which the term *narrative* has been used in the study of the New Testament has been the discovery of narratives or *stories* that have influenced the New Testament writers. Some scholars have discerned the influence of stories beneath the surface of the New Testament writings. The stories of creation and Adam, of Abraham and the patriarchs, of the exodus, kingship and exile, and of the promised coming messiah have informed and shaped the thinking of the writers and the writings as we have them. Sometimes these stories are obvious (for example, the story of Abraham in Romans 4 and Galatians 3–4). At other places the story is beneath the surface, and their presence and influence is debated (Do the stories of Adam's disobedience or of

---

9. Rhoads, Dewey, and Mitchie, *Mark as Story,* 146.
10. Resseguie, *Narrative Criticism,* 449 n. 22.
11. Parry, "Narrative Criticism," 528–31.

the Servant of Isaiah 53 form the background of Paul's thought in Phil 2:6–8?).[12] This is not so much the emphasis on the narrative shape of a passage (plot, character, point of view, etc.) as the narratives that have shaped the passage (creation, exodus, exile, etc.). It is this latter narrative critical study of the New Testament that is the primary focus of the present book. Is it possible that discernible narratives, which informed and shaped an author's writing of a text, offer fresh perspective on long-debated problems in New Testament textual criticism? Can the clarity gained on the textual-critical front in turn help the interpreter to a richer understanding of the passage in which the textual variation appears? To conduct this inquiry it will be important to review recent developments in three areas: New Testament Textual Criticism, The use of the Old Testament in the New Testament, and the Narrative Critical studies of the New Testament. Following these three preliminary explorations, we will study a number of textual critical problems, some of which continue to be debated. My hope is that the study of the *story* may give new perspective for decisions on the *text*, and that a new confidence regarding the *text* my lead to a better understanding of the *story*.

## NEW DIRECTIONS IN NEW TESTAMENT TEXTUAL CRITICISM

In recent years there have been significant developments in the discipline of New Testament textual criticism. The traditional goal in studying the textual tradition has been to recover the original text of the New Testament. But in the latter half of the twentieth century a second goal has begun to emerge. Students of the text have shifted their focus from the establishment of the original text to an emphasis on the historical and social climate that led to the growth of textual variations in the formative period of the second and third centuries. This focus on the early church context in which the text was copied and changed has offered new life to the discipline, attracting wider interest and growing debate. Several studies illustrate this important development in textual criticism.

In 1966 Eldon Jay Epp published his full-length study, *The Theological Tendency of Codex Bezae Cantabrigiensis in Acts*.[13] Epp argued that the distinctive text of this important fifth century manuscript showed evidence of an anti-Judaic bias and tendency on the part of its

---

12. Hawthorne and Martin, *Philippians*, 119.
13. Epp, *Theological Tendency*.

scribe, a tendency he shared with other representatives of the early so-called "Western" text of Acts. Epp's work built on the research of others and attracted a number of skeptical reviews.[14] But the value of his study was to set the stage for major works by Bart Ehrman and David Parker. Their work would chart a whole new course in the study of New Testament textual criticism. Epp, Ehrman, and Parker concentrated not so much on discovering the original text as on discerning the context and theological motives for the changes to the text in the early church.

The publication of Bart Ehrman's *The Orthodox Corruption of Scripture* in 1993 was a landmark in the study of the text of the New Testament. Ehrman's major thesis is that proto-orthodox scribes of the second and third centuries sometimes "altered their sacred texts to make them *say* what they were already known to *mean*."[15] Subsequently Ehrman has published other books in which he has argued this thesis with less technical data for a broader audience. His book *Lost Christianities* made Ehrman's arguments more accessible to a general readership, and his 2005 *Misquoting Jesus* has become a runaway bestseller.[16]

The theological issue on which Ehrman focuses his attention is the nature of Jesus Christ. Was he fully human? Was he really God? These issues were hotly debated in the second and third centuries. The early orthodox Christian leaders (whom Ehrman calls "proto-orthodox") found themselves in intense debate with groups and their teachers whom they called heretical. And Ehrman argues that under the pressure of these debates the proto-orthodox scribes altered their sacred texts intentionally at places where the New Testament seemed to support the teaching of a heretical group, and seemed to be potentially embarrassing for their own view. Ehrman notes several groups in particular. There were the *Adoptionists*, who believed that Jesus was not always the Son of God, but was adopted by God as Son at his baptism. There were the *Docetics,* who taught that Jesus was God and only appeared to be human. Since Jesus was God, they argued, he could not really be a man. He rather came to earth in the appearance of human flesh. A third group was the *Separationists.* They were so called because they separated Jesus and Christ. According to these teachers Christ and Jesus were two separate entities. They taught that the human Jesus was temporarily indwelt

---

14. Epp, *Perspectives,* 722 n. 84.
15. Ehrman, *Orthodox Corruption,* 276.
16. Ehrman, *Lost Christianities, Misquoting Jesus.*

by the divine being, Christ, enabling him to perform his miracles and deliver his teachings. But according to Ehrman, these separationists taught that at Jesus' death, "the Christ abandoned him, forcing him to face his crucifixion alone."[17] A fourth group studied by Ehrman were called *Patripassianists*. These second/third century teachers believed that the Father actually suffered when Jesus died on the cross. Thus they blurred the distinction between the Father and the Son. Ehrman studied a number of textual variations in the manuscript tradition of the New Testament and concluded that the pressure of controversy led the early proto-orthodox scribes to make alterations to their texts, in order to make them support the orthodox view, and to make them less susceptible to use by these heretical groups.

Ehrman argued that a number of variations within the textual tradition of the New Testament could be explained as orthodox corruptions for dogmatic purposes. Four of the most important textual variations, which Ehrman discusses extensively, are presented here as illustrations of his thesis. All four will be discussed in the following study.

LUKE 3:22. At Luke's report of the Father's voice at the baptism some manuscripts read, "You are my son, today I have begotten you." Ehrman asserts that this form of the text was what Luke originally wrote. But this form was very valuable to the Adoptionists, suggesting that it was at the baptism of Jesus that God adopted Jesus as his son, and therefore the proto-orthodox scribes altered the text to read like Matthew and Mark: "You are my beloved son in whom I am well-pleased."[18]

MARK 15:34. Mark records the cry of dereliction on the cross, "My God, My God, why have you forsaken me?" Ehrman argues that this is the original form of the verse. But it is easy to see how readily this verse might be used by the separationists, who believed that Christ came upon Jesus at his baptism and left him at his crucifixion. So, Ehrman argues, the reading of a few manuscripts "Why have you *mocked* me" represents the efforts of proto-orthodox scribes to ensure that the text supported orthodoxy and did not promote the heretical separationist views.[19]

17. Ehrman, *Misquoting Jesus*, 170.
18. Ehrman, *Orthodox Corruption*, 62 67, 142–43; *Lost Christianities*, 222–23; *Misquoting Jesus*, 160–61.
19. Ehrman, *Orthodox Corruption*, 143–45; *Lost Christianities*, 224–25; *Misquoting Jesus*, 172–73.

LUKE 22:43–44. This passage, which describes Jesus' bloody sweat in the garden of Gethsemane, is found in some manuscripts, but not in others. Ehrman argues that it was not original with Luke, but was added later by proto-orthodox scribes who were eager to assert against the teaching of the docetics that Jesus was really human.[20]

ACTS 20:28. The verse refers to "the church of God, which he purchased with his own blood." Ehrman argued that this verse could be taken by the patripassianists to refer to God shedding blood. To avoid such an interpretation, he asserts, the proto-orthodox scribes altered the text to read, "the church of the Lord." This would refer unambiguously to the Lord Jesus, rather than to the Father as the one who shed blood.[21]

Ehrman's work has been highly praised by many reviewers. Among them was David Parker, who built on Ehrman's work in his important study, *The Living Text of the Gospels*. Ehrman's focus was not on the quest for the original text of the New Testament, but rather on "subsequent forms of the text for understanding the history of exegesis."[22] Parker went a step further in asserting, "There is no original text, there are just different texts from different stages of production."[23] Parker's detailed study of the sayings of Jesus on marriage and divorce led him to conclude that the recovery of the original sayings of Jesus is impossible. What is available, he asserts, is not the original texts but "a collection of interpretive rewritings of the tradition."[24] Parker points to two facts,

> That the Gospel texts exist only in a manuscript tradition, and that from the beginning the text grew freely. It is from these facts that all questions of interpretation and all theological formulations must start. Concepts of biblical inspiration, or any other doctrinal formulations, which fail to take account of these two key facts are based on *a priori* theorizing or prejudice, and not on the actual character of the writings.[25]

---

20. Ehrman, *Orthodox Corruption*, 187–94; *Lost Christianities*, 225–26; *Misquoting Jesus*, 139–44, 164–65.
21. Ehrman, *Orthodox Corruption*, 87–88.
22. Ibid., 29.
23. Parker, *Living Text*, 4.
24. Ibid., 92–93.
25. Ibid., 203.

For Epp, Ehrman, and Parker, the textual variants tell a story. They are a window into the life of the second and third century church, and reflect the theological and ethical controversies that raged at that time.[26] The purpose of this study is to focus on another *story* that can help us to understand the history of the text, and offer new perspective on some of the textual variants that are still debated. Undoubtedly some of the variations in the New Testament manuscript tradition are best explained as intentional changes made by early scribes. But many of the variants for which intentional corruption is alleged may be explained as having arisen accidentally. For some of the variations the new insights gained from a narrative critical approach to the New Testament can offer a more satisfying alternative. A better appreciation of the *story* as understood by the New Testament writers can offer a fresh approach to long-standing text-critical problems.

## THE OLD TESTAMENT IN THE NEW TESTAMENT

The four examples cited above all occur in passages that quote or allude to the Old Testament or the scriptures of Israel. The study of the use of the Old Testament in the New Testament has developed over the last half century, and has an important bearing on our study of textual variations. Beginning with C. H. Dodd's landmark book *According to the Scriptures*,[27] a number of studies have refined our understanding of how the language and thought of the Jewish scriptures has shaped the writings of the New Testament. Early pioneering books focused on the use of the Old Testament by Matthew,[28] Paul,[29] and the use of scripture in the development of New Testament apologetic.[30] These studies confirmed and developed the sense that in the New Testament's use of the Old Testament we could discern what C. H. Dodd called "the substructure of New Testament theology."[31] The pioneering work by Richard B. Hays, *Echoes of Scripture in the Letters of Paul*, made clear the need for greater attention not only to the quotations and clear allusions to the scriptures

---

26. Ehrman, "Text as Window," 361–79.
27. Dodd, *According to the Scriptures*.
28. Stendahl, *School of St. Matthew*.
29. Ellis, *Paul's Use of the Old Testament*.
30. Lindars, *New Testament Apologetic*.
31. C. H. Dodd, in the subtitle of *According to the Scriptures*.

of Israel in the New Testament writings, but also the *echoes,* a word or phrase imbedded in the a gospel or letter which evoked a much larger context, known and understood by writer and readers. These are but a few of the spate of studies that have appeared on the subject. Indeed this area of research has received so much attention in recent years that it has warranted a large one-volume commentary devoted to the use of the Old Testament in the New Testament.[32]

It is surprising, therefore, to see how little this line of intertextual study has been appropriated by New Testament textual critics. The interest has not developed further than possible evidence of assimilation of New Testament passages to the Old Testament text being cited, or vise-versa. To give examples from the three important studies cited above, In Epp's collected essays, entitled *Perspectives on New Testament Textual Criticism,* one finds a meager list of Hebrew Bible (Old Testament) passages in the index, and most of these are from a list of quotations in Coptic MS G67, or in the discussion of Jewish and Christian manuscripts at Oxyrhynchus.[33] David Parker's *The Living Text of the Gospels* gives only five Old Testament references in the index,[34] and Bart Ehrman's index in *The Orthodox Corruption of Scripture* lists no Old Testament references.[35] Some Old Testament references are sprinkled throughout the book, but on the whole there is a clear tone-deafness to intertextuality and its possible bearing on text-critical issues.

Furthermore, it is surprising that New Testament textual critics have not been more alert to the developments in the textual criticism of the Hebrew Bible. By contrast, Emanuel Tov, in his *Textual Criticism of the Hebrew Bible,* reviews many of the principles practiced by his New Testament counterparts, and takes seriously their relevance for his own study.[36] Since the developments in the New Testament text, especially where there is a quotation, allusion or echo of the Old Testament, are part of a larger story of the development of the text of the Jewish scriptures, co-ordination of the two disciplines is essential. The following studies seek to be fully alert both to the use of the Old Testament in the New Testament and the textual transmission of the Hebrew Bible,

---

32. Beale and Carson, eds., *Commentary on the New Testament.*
33. Epp, *Perspectives,* 882.
34. Parker, *Living Text,* 214.
35. Ehrman, *Orthodox Corruption,* 303.
36. Tov, *Textual Criticism of the Hebrew Bible,* 302.

Septuagint and versions. The dividends for New Testament study can hardly be overstated.

## NARRATIVE CRITICISM AND THE NEW TESTAMENT

Narrative criticism is relatively new to biblical studies, but the number of scholars applying its insights to the New Testament has grown steadily.[37] Major impetus was given to this line of study by the seminal work by Hans Frei, *The Eclipse of the Biblical Narrative*.[38] Frei argued that for pre-critical readers the Bible was read as an over-reaching, continuous narrative. This "storied" feature of the text was overshadowed or eclipsed in the eighteenth and nineteenth centuries as modern critical scholarship approached the biblical text with different assumptions and treated it as a source of timeless truths and moral precepts rather than as story. Thus a vital element of the text was lost by its modern interpreters. Yet this narrative, this story of God and his people, was fundamental to the biblical writers' assumptions and approach. One of the early books that applied narrative critical insight to the interpretation of particular New Testament passages was Richard B. Hays, *The Faith of Jesus Christ*.[39] Hays focused on the story of Jesus as a creative feature in Paul's theology. He argued that the phrase "the faith of Jesus Christ" does not mean faith in Jesus Christ, but the faithfulness of Jesus Christ. Scholars remain divided as to whether "the faith of Jesus Christ" should be taken as a subjective genitive (Christ's faithfulness) or an objective genitive (our faith in Jesus Christ),[40] but Hays' study demonstrated how the narrative beneath the text has helped to shape Paul's argument in Galatians. Hays' subsequent book *Echoes of Scripture in the Letters of Paul* builds on his earlier work on the narrative character of Paul's theology.[41] As noted above, since mid-century there had been a growing body of study on the use of the Old Testament in the New. The work of C. H. Dodd, Krister Stendahl,

---

37. For an overview see the first chapter of Greene-McCreight, *Feminist Reconstructions*.

38. Frei, *Eclipse of the Biblical Narrative*.

39. Hays, *Faith of Jesus Christ*. Longenecker, *Narrative Dynamics*, for developments in Pauline studies.

40. Bird and Sprinkle, *Faith of Jesus Christ*.

41. Hays, *Echoes of Scripture in the Letters of Paul*, See also Hays' recent collection of essays, *The Conversion of the Imagination*, in which Hays responds to some of the critique of his approach in *Echoes*.

and E. Earl Ellis, to name just a few leading studies, had explored the various different aspects of the quotations and clear allusions to the Old Testament in the New Testament writings.[42] In *Echoes*, Hays looks beyond quotations and allusions to the way in which Old Testament stories and passages exercise a creative role in Paul's writings. So, for example, when Paul cites Ps 143:2 in Rom 3:20 Hays asserts:

> The Psalm is not adduced as a proof of Paul's assertion, but his assertion echoes the Psalm, activating Israel's canonical memory. A reader formed spiritually by the Psalter, with or without recognizing the specific allusion, will know already that before God no one can claim to be justified.[43]

Hays notes the following various criteria whereby echoes can be discerned in the New Testament: availability, volume, recurrence, thematic coherence, historical plausibility, history of interpretation, and satisfaction.[44] He demonstrates that Paul is not merely echoing a verse of the Psalm, but that Psalm 143, read as a whole, undergirds the logic of Rom 3, that is, it provides the *story* of Romans 3. "By following the echoes of Psalm 143," Hays writes, "we can rediscover the scriptural idea of God's saving justice as the foundation of Paul's argument in Romans."[45] Thus Romans 3 is not, as is sometimes assumed, a series of loosely joined paragraphs, bolstered by proof texts, but the *story* of God's saving justice. Among the many who have benefited from and built on Hays' work is Ben Witherington III, who notes "Paul's allusive handling of Scripture shows that he believed one needs to know the whole story to appreciate the parts."[46]

Another pioneer in the narrative critical study of the New Testament is N. T. Wright. Wright's groundbreaking book, *The New Testament and the People of God*, published in 1992 was the first volume in a projected six volume series entitled *Christian Origins and the Question of God*.[47] He applies narrative critical insights to the whole of the New Testament

---

42. Dodd, *According to the Scriptures*; Stendahl, *School of Matthew*; Ellis, *Paul's use of the Old Testament*.

43. Hays, *Echoes*, 51.

44. Hays, *Echoes*, 29–32; *Conversion*, 34–45.

45. Hays, *Echoes*, 53.

46. Witherington III, *The Paul Quest*, 231.

47. So far three volumes have appeared: *The New Testament and the People of God*, *Jesus and the Victory of God*, and *The Resurrection of the Son of God*.

in its second-temple Jewish and Greco-Roman context. Stories, Wright argues, express worldviews which issue in both symbol and praxis. The New Testament writers share a common story with all other Jewish groups of the second temple period. The outlines of that story were: There is one God who created the world, a creation gone wrong in the sin of Adam. God has called to himself a covenant people, rescued them from bondage in Egypt, and established them in the land of promise. But due to their unfaithfulness, that people is now in exile. But God is going to intervene to restore his people to their inheritance. The Christians shared and told this story, but added their own ending. In Jesus Christ, and especially his death and resurrection, God has already acted to redeem his people.[48] Wright's application of this narrative perspective to the New Testament has resulted in a fresh reading of a number of New Testament passages. So, for example, the parable of the sower (Mark 4), which has been subjected to a wide variety of interpretations, appears in a different light when considered in the broader narrative of God and his dealings with his people. According to Wright, "The parable tells the story of Israel, particularly the return from exile, with a paradoxical conclusion, and it tells the story of Jesus' ministry, as the fulfillment of that larger story, with a paradoxical outcome."[49] The "seed," Wright argues, is a metaphor for the true Israel, who will be vindicated when her god finally acts, "sown" again in her own land. "For someone announcing the kingdom to tell a story about the seed being sown, then, would be to say: the remnant is now returning. The exile is over."[50]

Wright's narrative critical approach to this and many other New Testament passages has produced lively debate.[51] The work of Wright, Hays and others is having an increasing influence in New Testament studies and across the theological disciplines. Full-length monographs have appeared applying the work of Hays and Wright to other writings of the New Testament.[52] Moreover, this perspective has had a broad in-

48. A helpful introduction and summary of Wright's approach can be found in his short study, *The Challenge of Jesus*.

49. Wright, *Jesus and the Victory of God*, 230.

50. Ibid., 230–39.

51. See for example the essays in Carey C. Newman, ed. *Jesus and the Restoration of Israel*.

52. Watts, *Isaiah's New Exodus in Mark*; Pao, *Acts and the Isaianic New Exodus*; Wagner, *Heralds of the Good News*; and Mbuvi, *Temple, Exile and Identity in 1 Peter*. For an example of similar developments in Old Testament study see Enns, *Exodus Retold*, who builds on the work of Michael Fishbane, *Biblical Interpretation in Ancient Israel*.

fluence in other theological disciplines. It is not uncommon to encounter a statement like that in the recent important book on missiology by Christopher H. J. Wright, entitled *The Mission of God*, "It is in Christ crucified and risen that we find the focal point of the whole Bible's grand narrative."[53]

The purpose of this book is to argue that the textual critic can be both beneficiary and contributor to the narrative critical approach to the New Testament. Thus far, narrative critical discussions of New Testament passages have usually bypassed or ignored textual critical issues in the discussion of specific passages. There have been some notable exceptions. For example, Richard Hays takes seriously the textual critical issues at Rom 4:1 in his discussion of the narrative dynamic of the whole section in Romans.[54] He thus shows an awareness of the critical importance of textual issues for exegesis in general and narrative critical construal in particular. But there is much work to be done in this area, which will both shed light on textual critical issues that continue to be debated, and offer fresh perspective for narrative critical interpretation.

Each of the following chapters explores a New Testament textual variation that is still being debated. Each discussion stands on its own, but there is a common factor in that all involve variations within quotations, allusions or echoes of the Old Testament in the New. Taken as a whole, I hope these essays will demonstrate that there are rich dividends for those who consider *text* and *story* together.

## ABOUT THE BOOK

Each of the ten chapters in this book, with the exception of the first, follows the same structure. Their shape is determined by the criteria employed by New Testament textual critics in their evaluation of variant readings. Priority is given to the evidence in the *manuscript tradition*, but in most cases the support for one reading or another is not so strong as to settle the textual question. *Internal considerations*, such as the style, theology, and literary art of an author must also be studied carefully. *Transcriptional probabilities*, that is, judgments about what scribes were likely to have done in the course of copying, are a vital part of the inquiry. A determination must be made concerning which reading best

---

53. Wright, *Mission of God*, 535.
54. Hays, *Echoes*, 54; *Conversion*, 61–84.

explains the rise of the alternatives in the transmission of the text. But when each of these factors has been considered in their turn the textual question may still not be settled. I believe that this is the case with each of the verses I have selected for study. We then turn our attention to *narrative features* of the text. Each one of the verses considered incorporates a quotation, allusion or echo of the Old Testament, and I believe that careful study of these citations from the scriptures of Israel can offer fresh evidence and perspective for the solution of the textual question. These scripture references, often in combination with others, undergird and interpret the story of God and his people, which the New Testament writers believed had reached its climax in the life, death, resurrection and exaltation of Jesus. I conclude each essay with a brief sketch of the *Transmission History* of the text indicated by my proposal.

Chapter 1, on Romans 8:28, was originally published in the *Journal of Theological Studies* in 1995, and is reproduced[55] without alteration to illustrate how I first discovered that broader narrative features, indicated by an echo of the Old Testament, can be valuable both for understanding the writing in which it is found, and also for establishing the text. The note was published before I had read Jon D. Levenson's *The Death and Resurrection of the Beloved Son*. Levenson's study, and in particular his treatment of the Joseph story (Genesis 37–50) "the longest and most intricate exemplar of the narrative of the death and resurrection of the beloved son,"[56] gives added support to the conclusions I drew in this short note. But I had been thinking about how the narrative of scripture shapes the New Testament re-telling of the story of God and his people long before the production of my 1995 publication. Even as a graduate student in the 1970's, under the guidance of my two supervisors, G. D. Kilpatrick and Geza Vermes, I had seen the value of broader narrative considerations for both textual and interpretive issues in New Testament study.[57]

Many people have helped me in the production of this book. I am grateful to James Gregory for substantive and technical assistance throughout this project. To my readers, Prof. J. K. Elliott, Prof. Dale Liid, The Rev. Dr. Kathryn Greene-McCreight, Dr. David R. Vinson and Karen Bolte, I owe a debt of gratitude for their incisive comments. Shawn

---

55. With kind permission.
56. Levenson, *Death and Resurrection*, 143.
57. Wright, *Justification*, 157.

McCain assembled the bibliography. Many mistakes have been avoided due to their efforts. Those that remain are my responsibility, not theirs. I am grateful also to Prof. N. T. Wright for reading and commenting on the chapter on Mark 9:29, and to Dr. J. Harold Ellens for publishing the last chapter on the text of Luke 4:18 in his three volume work, *The Healing Power of Spirituality*.[58] Dr. David Instone-Brewer also read this chapter and offered valuable comments on interpretive techniques and assumptions in Judaism in the Second Temple period. His book on this subject is essential reading for anyone exploring scripture interpretation in the time of Jesus.[59] I am grateful to Dr. Christopher Spinks and the editorial team at Wipf and Stock for their efficient and courteous assistance in seeing this book through the publication process.

I offer these essays as an encouragement to further conversation, with the hope that they will stimulate rather than stifle discussion. If they can foster the further coordination of textual criticism, exegesis and theology, I will consider the effort to be worthwhile. I hope also that they will generate a deepened sense of the storied nature of the text the church reads as scripture.

---

58. Rodgers, "Luke 4:18: 'To Heal the Brokenhearted,'" 162–69.

59. Instone-Brewer, *Techniques and Assumptions*.

# 1

## Romans 8:28

ROMANS 8:28 IS ONE of the best-known and best loved verses in the New Testament. The several ways of reading the text reflect a much-discussed textual *crux interpretum*. In the King James Version the verse reads, "All things work together for good . . ." This translation depends on the Greek text found in the majority of manuscripts in which "all things" (πάντα) is usually taken as the subject of "works" (συνεργεῖ). Some who continue to favor this reading give the sense of "co-operate" to the verb. This way of reading the text still commends itself to a number of modern commentators including Michel, Käsemann, Barrett, Cranfield, Dunn, and Fitzmyer.

The Revised Standard Version and the New International Version make "God" the subject, i.e., "In all things God works . . ." This is the reading found in some of the oldest manuscripts including P[46] (which reads πᾶν for πάντα), Codex Vaticanus (B), and Codex Alexandrinus (A), where the word "God" (ὁ Θεός) follows the verb "works." It was printed in brackets by Westcott and Hort in their 1881 edition of the Greek New Testament. Sanday and Headlam championed this reading in their 1898 commentary. They have been followed in this century by Barth, Goodspeed, and Moffatt. It is interesting to note that the New Revised Standard Version does not follow its predecessor, but reads "All things work . . ." Most would follow Käsemann in dubbing the reading "God" "an edifying emendation."[1]

A third interpretation of the *crux*, one involving a conjecture, has commended itself to scholars. Some take "the Spirit" to be the subject of "work together." This view, popularized in the New English Bible, was

---

1. Käsemann, *Romans*, 243.

developed by J. P. Wilson.[2] Criticisms of this view have centered on the resort to conjecture when two readings exist which make clear sense and are well supported. Critics also point out that although "the Spirit" is the subject of v. 26, "God" is the subject of v. 27. It is most natural, then, to read v. 28 with "God" as the subject.

Among those supporting the shorter reading which omits "God " (ὁ Θεός) is J. A. T. Robinson who wrote, "There is no good reason *ho theos* (God) should have dropped out, though good reason for adding it as the subject to the verb "work together" for those who found it impossible to believe that "all things could be the subject."[3] But Robinson has overlooked the matters of style and literary fashions in the transmission of the text. While some scribes may have been tempted to insert God (ὁ Θεός) in the text of Rom 8:28 "to make the matter unambiguous,"[4] others would be tempted to remove it in order to improve the style of a sentence that had already used the name "God." What is the evidence for this view?

A movement grew up in literary circles of the second century CE that valued the style of the Attic writers. While copyists did not systematically revise the works of authors they were copying, a tendency to improve style can be found in both pagan and biblical texts of the period.[5] One of the habits of the early scribes with an eye on style was to cut down on repetition. While New Testament authors were generally insensitive to repetition of words in the same sentence, the scribes were not. In general, their rule of thumb, in imitation of Attic authors, was that "the better style would be usually the briefer."[6] And there is an additional factor that, in contrast to classical texts, "the Bible and other texts which were read aloud suffered more severely from linguistic and stylistic correction."[7] It is easy to see how the subject "God" at Rom 8:28 could have been removed, especially as "God" (ὁ Θεός) is the most frequently used substantive word in Romans.[8] The scribe, certain of the subject, may have been more sensitive to the repetition than to the

---

2. Wilson, "Romans viii 28," 110–11, followed by Dodd, Black, and Best.
3. Robinson, *Wrestling*, 104.
4. Cranfield, *Romans*, 1, 426.
5. Kilpatrick, *Principles and Practice*, 63–72.
6. Ibid., 72.
7. Ibid.
8. Morris, "The Theme" 250; Fitzmyer, *Romans*, 104.

grammatical ambiguity he introduced. Of course, the other way of improving the style, by eliminating the repetition, would be to change the "God" (Θεόν) in the verse to "him" (αὐτόν). We note that this reading is found in Origen *de Oratione* XXXIX. 19. (ὁ θεὸς, ὁ τοῖς ἀγαπῶσιν αὐτὸν πάντα συνεργῶν εἰς ἀγαθόν). This may represent an attempt to remedy the style without introducing theological ambiguity A similar situation may be noted at Rom 1:28 where "God" (ὁ Θεός) is omitted by ℵ* A pc. Cranfield takes this as an accidental omission, possibly due to the "God" (θεόν) earlier in the verse.[9] It may not be accidental.

Nonetheless, not all scribes yielded to the temptation. If there was a movement toward "stylistic correctness" in the second century, the scribe(s) whose manuscripts stand behind P46 A B, etc. valued "theological correctness" all the more. They resisted the trend of the culture to conform the biblical text to the Attic style, with the lure of making it more "relevant," acceptable, and accessible to the cultured people of their day. They were determined to retain and to present what they found in the text of Paul, however out of fashion the style might be. And this is all the more remarkable when we consider that the very manuscripts which have the longer text with its repetition are Alexandrian witnesses, coming from the corner of the world especially known for such stylistic revision! These are the very manuscripts in which we would expect the shorter text. In this connection, it is instructive to note the figures gleaned by M. Silva in his collation of the earliest manuscripts of Galatians. Silva found that

> Using UBS³/Nestle²⁶ as the collation base "P⁴⁶ is 45 words shorter than UBS³, ℵ 14 shorter, B six words shorter. A, on the other hand is the earliest Greek text that is longer (by 9 words) than UBS³."[10]

In the case of P⁴⁶ and B the scribes appear to have abandoned their usual practice and habit at Rom 8:28.

But there is another consideration which may help us with our textual question. Among the parallels cited as giving a similar thought to that of Rom 8:28 is Gen 50:20. Indeed Cranfield cites this as the primary parallel.[11] It does not seem too far-fetched to overhear at Rom 8:28 a conscious echo of Gen 50:20. Where the LXX reads "but God intended

---

9. Cranfield, *Romans*, 1, 128.
10. Silva, "Text of Galatians," 17–25.
11. Cranfield, *Romans*, 1, 429 n. 1.

good for me." (ὁ δὲ Θεὸς ἐβουλεύσατο περὶ ἐμοῦ εἰς ἀγαθά). Such a suggestion is supported by the thesis of R. B. Hays,[12] in which special attention is given to "intertextual echoes" in the Pauline letters. Hays defined this phenomenon of intertextuality as "the imbedding of fragments of an earlier text within a later one."[13] Intertextual echoes are subtler than quotations or allusions, and Hays offers criteria for testing a proposed echo in a Pauline letter. He cites, for example, availability, volume, recurrence and satisfaction. Another criterion he gives is "thematic coherence." Hays asks:

> How well does the alleged echo fit into the line of argument that Paul is developing? Is its meaning effect consonant with other quotations in the same letter or elsewhere in the Pauline corpus? Do the images and ideas of the proposed precursor text illuminate Paul's argument?[14]

In answering these questions with regard to Rom 8:28, it is pertinent to note what follows in Gen 50:20, and to compare it to what follows in Romans 9–11. Genesis 50:20 reads, "Even though you intended to do harm to me, God intended it for good, in order to preserve a numerous people, as he is doing today." The verse comes at the end of the story in which Joseph was sold by his brothers into Egypt, and endured slavery and imprisonment, before he is raised up to become the deliverer of both nations and his own brothers in time of famine. A similar pattern may be noted in Romans 9–11, where Israel has fallen away and the Gentiles have become partakers of God's blessings. Through this process Israel will also be saved, as Paul writes to Gentile Christians:

> Just as you were once disobedient, but have now received mercy because of their disobedience, so they have now been disobedient, in order that by the mercy shown to you, they too may now receive mercy." (Rom 11:30–31)

Like Joseph, Jesus and his message were rejected by his own people but accepted among the Gentiles. By a similar surprising twist Israel is to be restored. In both cases "God meant it for good."

If at Romans 8:28 there is an echo of Gen 50:20, which continues to reverberate through the themes of Romans 9–11, it is significant that the

---

12. Hays, *Echoes*.
13. Ibid., 14.
14. Ibid., 30.

subject of the echoed clause is "God" (ὁ Θεός). This corroborates what I have argued on other grounds with regard to the text.[15]

---

15. Reprinted *JTS* 46 (1995) 547-50, with kind permission of Oxford University Press.

# 2

# Luke 3:22

THE ACCOUNT OF THE baptism of Jesus in the Gospel of Luke ends with the citation of the voice from heaven, "You are my Son, the Beloved; with you I am well-pleased" (Luke 3:22). At least that is what we read in the NRSV, and we find parallels with slightly different wording in Matthew and Mark, and an echo of the voice in the Gospel of John (Matt 3:17; Mark 1:11; John 1:34). But in Luke the NRSV footnote reads, "Other ancient authorities read, 'You are my Son, today I have begotten you.'" This alternative reading is found in the fifth century Greek/Latin bilingual manuscript Codex Bezae Catabrigiensis, or Codex D, in some old Latin manuscripts of Luke, and in some early Christian writers, notably Justin Martyr (*Dialogue with Trypho* 88). Our printed texts and translations adopt the reading of the bulk of Greek manuscripts, but the D reading has received renewed attention in recent years, and some have argued that it is what Luke originally wrote. In particular, Bart D. Ehrman has argued that the alternative text, "You are my Son, today I have begotten you," is originally what Luke wrote, and under the pressure of controversy with adoptionist teachers in the second and third centuries, it was changed by proto-orthodox scribes to conform to Mark and Matthew and to avoid an adoptionist construal.[1] Summarizing his argument in his recent revision of Bruce M. Metzger's classic, *The Text of the New Testament*, Ehrman writes:

> In a wide range of early patristic sources of the second and third centuries the voice is said to have quoted Ps 2.7: "You are my Son, today I have begotten you." This latter form of the text, of course, could have proved useful to those holding adoptionistic views, for it could be construed to say that it was at Jesus' baptism that

1. Ehrman, *Orthodox Corruption*, 62–67.

he became God's son. It may well be, then, that the form of text attested in the majority of witnesses, in this case, represents an anti-adoptionistic corruption of the original.[2]

Ehrman builds an impressive case for his contention that the alternate reading at Luke 3:22 is the original reading. He shows that it is not "an error introduced by an unusually aberrant witness" (D), which he argues is "one of the last witnesses to preserve it." Nor is it merely a "Western" variant without adequate attestation. Rather the reading is "virtually the only reading to be found; down to the sixth century it occurs in witnesses as far-flung as Asia Minor, Palestine, Alexandria, North Africa, Rome, Gaul and Spain."[3]

## MANUSCRIPT SUPPORT

Most commentators follow our printed modern editions and translations. For example, J. A. Fitzmyer wrote, "Despite the importance of Codex Bezae, this is not the best attested reading."[4] But Ehrman's arguments deserve careful consideration, and his work on Luke 3:22 is a model of independent judgment on text-critical questions. In subsequent chapters I shall be arguing in several instances that the more poorly attested reading in the manuscript tradition is the original reading. Textual questions cannot simply be settled by appealing to the "oldest and best" manuscripts. That this is the case is clearly seen by the fact that on a number of occasions the United Bible Societies committee has chosen a reading that is not supported by any of the early papyri and by none of the great uncial manuscripts (ℵ A B etc).[5] These are usually regarded as our "oldest and best" manuscripts. For example, editors have preferred the reading *we have peace* at Rom 5:1, even though it has slender manuscript support, and it is not found in ℵ, B, etc. The committee judged that "internal evidence must take precedence here."[6] Decisions on textual questions need to consider not only the external criteria (the date, quality and geographical spread of manuscript support) but also

---

2. Metzger and Ehrman, *Text of the New Testament*, 285-86.

3. Ehrman, *Othodox Corruption*, 62-63. For a popular discussion, accessible to the non-specialist see Ehrman, *Misquoting Jesus*, 158-61.

4. Fitzmyer, *Luke I-IX*, 485.

5. Rodgers, "The New Eclecticism," 391 for a list of those found in UBS³. See appendix, p.107.

6. Metzger, *Textual Commentary*, 452.

internal criteria (style and theology of an author) and transcriptional probabilities (why scribes would have changed a reading, either intentionally or accidentally). What Ehrman has shown is that the decision on the original text of Luke 3:22 cannot be made on the basis of manuscript evidence alone. Internal criteria, together with transcriptional probabilities must be given full consideration.

## TRANSCRIPTIONAL PROBABILITIES

After considering the manuscript support for both readings at Luke 3:22, the interpreter must consider what is the most plausible explanation for the change. Ehrman's argument that scribes of the second and third centuries would have changed the text to avoid an adoptionist construal is impressive. But all the transcriptional probabilities should be considered. Fitzmyer suggests that "Scribes familiar with the Greek Psalter would have substituted this quotation, derived from a psalm often interpreted in the early Christian centuries as 'messianic.'"[7] This particular possibility should be taken very seriously, since the psalms were regularly employed in early Christian worship, and their wording would have either been memorized or deeply embedded in the minds of early Christian scribes. On the other hand, it could be argued that the form of the voice at the baptism found in Matthew (with variation) and Mark (without variation) would have exercised a similar influence on scribes. This argument from harmonization is inconclusive as well.

We need also to consider the fact that Justin Martyr cites Ps 2:7 as the voice at the baptism in the mid-second century. So does Clement of Alexandria at the end of the century and Origen in the early third century. This suggests that these early Christian writers either did not feel the adoptionist overtones, in an age when the controversy on adoptionism was especially strong, or else they resisted changing the text, however embarrassing it might seem from their point of view.[8] Textual decisions on the basis of transcriptional probability are no less straightforward than those depending primarily on the external (manuscript) evidence.

---

7. Fitzmyer, *Luke I–IX*, 485.
8. Rodgers, review of Kim Haines-Eitzen, *Guardians of Letters*, 404–7.

## NARRATIVE CONSIDERATIONS

A fresh approach to the textual problem at Luke 3:22 may be found if we consider the text from a narrative critical standpoint, with special attention to the echoes of the Old Testament in the voice. In recent years commentators have been increasingly confident that the voice at the baptism in the synoptic gospels echoes three Old Testament texts: Ps 2:7; Isa 42:1–2; and Gen 22:2, 12, 16.[9] We will consider each text separately, study their combination in the voice at the baptism, and explore their bearing on the textual question at Luke 3:22.

Few would deny that the voice at the baptism (Matt 3:17, Mark 1:11, Luke 3:22) echoes Ps 2:7: "I will tell of the decree of the Lord: He said to me, 'You are my son; today I have begotten you.'"[10] Whether or not this psalm was given a messianic interpretation in pre-Christian Judaism, it certainly was a Messianic *testimonium* from the very earliest days of the Christian movement. C. H. Dodd, in his classic treatment, *According to the Scriptures*, lists Ps 2:7 first in his review of the most important Old Testament citations for New Testament writers.[11] The words are quoted by Paul in his speech at Antioch of Pisidia in Acts 13:32–33:

> And we bring you good news that what God promised
> to our ancestors
> he has fulfilled for us, their children, by raising Jesus;
> as also it is written
> in the second psalm,
> "You are my Son
> today I have begotten you."

We also find the words of Ps 2:7 quoted in Heb 1:5, here combined with other messianic testimonies:

> For to which of the angels did God ever say,
> "You are my Son;
> today I have begotten you"?

In Heb 5:5–6 the writer includes a citation from Ps 2:7 in his discussion of Jesus as the great high priest, and follows it with a citation of Ps 110:4:

---

9. For a proposal that John 1:34 (if we accept all the variants) also echoes all three Old Testament texts see Rodgers, "Text of John 1:34," 299–305.

10. A notable dissenter is Jeremias, *New Testament Theology*, 54, who argues that only Isa 42:1f is echoed in the voice at the baptism, and not Ps 2:7.

11. Dodd, *According to the Scriptures*, 31–32.

> So Christ did not glorify himself in becoming a high priest,
> but was appointed by the one who said to him,
> "You are my Son,
> today I have begotten you";
> As he says also in another place,
> "You are priest forever,
> according to the order of Melchizedek."

In addition to these quotations are the allusions and echoes of Ps 2:7 in the voice at the baptism, at the transfiguration of Jesus and in Nathaniel's exclamation in John 1:49. So we see that the verse was clearly understood as referring to God's anointed one, the Messiah, by the earliest Christians, and the echo at Luke 3:22 also carries this connotation.[12] Luke employs an echo of Ps 2:7 to present the baptism as Jesus' anointing as Messiah.

The second text echoed, or "foregrounded"[13] by the heavenly voice at Luke 3:22 is Isa 42:1. The Davidic king is anointed, not with oil, but with the Spirit, to commission and equip him for the ministry of the Servant sketched out in the Servant passages of Isa 40–55. The verbal resonance is found in the words "with you I am well-pleased." The wording here (εὐδόκησα) is closer to the MT (Masoretic Text) and the Greek translations, Theodotian and Aquila than to LXX (Septuagint), and is similar to the form in Matt 12:18, where Isa 42:1–4 is given as a formula quotation to affirm that Jesus fulfills the role of God's chosen servant:

> This was to fulfill what had been spoken through the prophet Isaiah:
> "Here is my servant, whom I have chosen,
> my beloved, with whom my soul is well pleased.
>
> (εἰς ὃν εὐδόκησεν ἡ ψυχή μου)
>
> I will put my Spirit upon him,
> and he will proclaim justice to the Gentiles.
> He will not wrangle or cry aloud,
> nor will anyone hear his voice in the streets.
> He will not break a bruised reed
> or quench a smoldering wick
> until he brings justice to victory.
> And in his name the Gentiles will hope."

---

12. Green, *Luke*, 186.
13. Ibid., 187.

The third text echoed in the voice at the baptism is Gen 22:2. The word "beloved" (ὁ ἀγαπητός) is taken by many to be drawn from the story of the near sacrifice of Isaac.

> After these things God tested Abraham. He said to him, "Abraham!" And he said, "Here I am." ²He said, "Take your son, your only son Isaac, whom you love, and go to the land of Moriah, and offer him there as a burnt-offering on one of the mountains that I shall show you."

The word *beloved* is repeated in verses 12 and 16. Long ago C. H. Turner commented that no passage of the LXX is more likely than Gen 22, in conjunction with Ps 2:7, to lie behind the thought of those who rendered into Greek the voice at the baptism.[14] The story of the near sacrifice of Isaac is recounted in Heb 11:17–19:

> By faith Abraham, when put to the test, offered up Isaac. He who had received the promises was ready to offer up his only son, of whom he had been told, "It is through Isaac that descendants shall be named for you." He considered the fact that God is able even to raise someone from the dead—and figuratively speaking, he received him back.

But scholars have also recognized echoes of Gen 22 in other New Testament passages. In particular, many see a reference to the story in Rom 8:32, "He who did not withhold his own son, but gave him up for all of us, will he not with him also give us everything else?"[15] Ever since Origen, an allusion to Gen 22:16 has been recognized in this verse. An echo of the Sacrifice of Isaac has also been detected in other New Testament passages: 1 Pet 1:20;[16] Acts 20:28.[17] Since the story was considerably important to Jews in the second temple period, especially those suffering persecution, it would not be surprising to find it influencing the New Testament writers as well.[18]

Each of these passages, then, Ps 2:7; Isa 42:1; and Gen 22:2, 12, 16, exercised an influence on the New Testament writers. But what calls for special attention is the combination of phrases from each of these texts

---

14. Turner, *St. Mark*, 13.
15. Dahl, "The Atonement," 15–29. See also Fitzmyer, *Romans*, 531.
16. LeDeaut, "Le Targum," 103–6.
17. See chapter 6 below.
18. For recent discussion see Vermes, *Changing Face*, 92–94.

in the voice at the baptism. Here is what we may call a *composite echo*, the combining of catch-phrases from two or more Old Testament passages in a New Testament context. The use of just one word, for example "beloved," or "only" (ὁ ἀγαπητός), was enough for the first century Jew, whether Palestinian or Hellenistic, to hear the clear echo of Genesis 22. It is important to consider both the background of such combination of texts and the theological significance in early Christianity of their combination.

Exploration of the background to the use of the Old Testament in the New Testament must consider how the Hebrew Bible was read, preached and expounded in the synagogue in the second temple period. This subject and its bearing on New Testament studies have been the material of careful studies over the years by E. Earle Ellis.[19] In an essay entitled "How the New Testament Uses the Old," Ellis gives a number of examples of how New Testament passages incorporate the "proem midrash pattern" of combining several Old Testament texts, often through the use of key words that connect these texts, which in turn interpret and illumine each other.[20] That pattern had the following form:

> The (Pentateuchal) text for the day.
> The second text, the proem or "opening" for the discourse.
> Exposition containing additional Old Testament citations, parables or other commentary and linked to the initial texts by catch-words.
> The final text, usually repeating or alluding to the text for the day.[21]

Normally the pattern would incorporate in the exposition texts from the law, the prophets and the writings (cf. Luke 24:44), drawn together because they were the readings for the day, or because they were suggested by a catchword. A good example offered by Ellis is Gal 4:21—5:1, where citations, allusions or echoes from all three sections of scripture may be detected. Some examples Ellis gives from the New Testament lack the pentateuchal text for the day, or fail to produce citations from all three parts of the Hebrew Bible. What Ellis has uncovered in the New Testament is fragments of the pattern, but it offers some very helpful clues for interpretation.

---

19. See especially the collection of essays of Ellis, *Prophecy and Hermeneutic*.

20. The essay originally appeared in Marshall, ed. *New Testament Interpretation*, 199–219.

21. Ellis, *New Testament Interpretation*, 203.

What is striking about the voice at the baptism is that it incorporates echoes from all three sections of the scriptures: the law, the prophets, and the writings. Moreover, the catchwords linking the passages together would have been either "son" (υἱός, παῖς) or "beloved" (ἀγαπητός), or both. In other words, in the voice at the baptism, the gospel writers appear to be practicing a common exegetical procedure, using very important texts for Christian teaching and apologetic. These texts were well enough known that the mere mention of the catchwords would be enough to evoke the whole passages. They are the tip of the iceberg, so to speak. That Luke uses the technique of one word evoking a whole story is clearly seen, for example, in Luke 9:31, where the word translated departure is exodus (τὴν ἔξοδον). Here is a whole story in a single word, which serves to "activate Israel's canonical memory,"[22] and evoke the whole passage, and not just isolated verses. We will explore this aspect of the subject in subsequent chapters. For the present discussion of the text of Luke 3:22 it is sufficient to notice that the printed text like Matthew and Luke participates in this rich exegetical activity, where the three Old Testament texts interpret each other. If Jesus is the anointed king of Psalm 2, that Messiahship is nuanced both by the career of the Servant (Isaiah 42) and the sacrifice prefigured in Genesis 22. This is a far more satisfactory and penetrating way of understanding the voice at the Baptism. Luke is participating in the same Christian prophetic exegesis as Matthew and Mark (and, I have argued, John as well). The story of Jesus the Son, the Servant, the Sacrifice, as understood according to the Scriptures, is the much more likely scenario for Luke 3:22, than a supposed late-second-century scribal paranoia concerning adoptionism.[23]

## TRANSMISSION HISTORY

The majority of manuscripts at Luke 3:22 read, "You are my Son, the Beloved, with you I am well pleased." It is probable that some early scribes were so familiar with Ps 2:7 that they inadvertently wrote "You are my son, today I have begotten you." The value of this Psalm verse as a testimony to Christ would mean that it continued to be cited by early

---

22. Hays, *Echoes*, 51.
23. That the earliest Christians would have heard echoes of these three Old Testament texts in the voice at the baptism in no way detracts from the likelihood that the report of the event was based on authentic eyewitness testimony. See Bauckham, *Eyewitnesses*.

Christian writers in connection with Jesus' baptism (Justin, *Dialogue with Trypho* 88, 103) even though the verse was potentially useful to Adoptionist heretics.

# 3

# Hebrews 2:9

Hebrews 2:9 contains the most famous textual problem in the letter. Most of the witnesses read: "But we see Jesus, who for a little while was made lower than the angels, now crowned with glory and honor because of the suffering of death, so that by the grace of God he might taste death for everyone." However, a few manuscripts and some early Christian writers read not "by the grace of God," (χάριτι θεοῦ) but "apart from God" (χωρὶς θεοῦ). To say that Jesus died "apart from God" is to say something very different than that he died "by the grace of God." In the first three editions of the United Bible Societies Greek New Testament the decision in favor of the printed reading, "by the grace of God," was given a {B} rating. This indicates that some scholars favor the less well-attested reading, "apart from God."[1] The fourth edition of UBS gives the decision an {A} rating, indicating general agreement among the members of the editorial committee.

Bruce Metzger notes in the *Textual Commentary* that the reading "apart from God" (χωρὶς θεοῦ) is read by "a rather large number of Fathers, both Eastern and Western."[2] Especially early and noteworthy among them is Origen, who knew both readings and noted that in his day, the early third century, "apart from God" was the reading of the majority of manuscripts known to him.[3] He was also reluctant to choose between the two readings, since he found spiritual value in both of them.[4]

---

1. Ehrman, *Orthodox Corruption*, 146–50.
2. Metzger, *Textual Commentary*, 594.
3. Ehrman, *Misquoting Jesus*, 145.
4. Metzger and Ehrman, *Text of the New Testament*, 200.

## MANUSCRIPT EVIDENCE

Those who consider the external criteria, or manuscript evidence, as the decisive factor in textual decisions will follow the view of the majority of commentators voiced by William L. Lane, "The textual support for the reading χάριτι θεοῦ (by the grace of God) . . . seems decisive."[5] All but three Greek manuscripts of Hebrews support this reading. Of these three manuscripts, 1739, a tenth-century minuscule manuscript, containing the Acts and epistles, deserves special notice.[6] Ehrman notes that 1739 represents "the conscientious transcription of a fourth century exemplar, whose text derives from a manuscript at least as ancient as our earliest papyri."[7] He also cites the judgment of Günther Zuntz that 1739 "represents a manuscript comparable, in age and quality, to P[46]."[8]

But the combination of this important witness, a number of Church fathers and versions, and the fact that "apart from God" appears to have been the reading of the majority of manuscripts in Origin's day is not enough to persuade most commentators. This, however, does not settle the matter. Lively debate has centered on both transcriptional probabilities and internal criteria (stylistic and theological considerations).

## TRANSCRIPTIONAL PROBABILITIES

It is easy to see how the textual variation could have arisen accidentally. The words for "by the grace of God" and "apart from God" are very similar in Greek. But in which direction would the change likely have taken place? Bart Ehrman argues rightly that the careless scribe would certainly have changed the less familiar and more troubling phrase to a more familiar and more agreeable one:

> Is a negligent or absentminded scribe likely to have changed his text by writing a word used *less* frequently in the New Testament (χωρὶς) or one used *more* frequently (χάριτι, four times as common)? Is he likely to have created a phrase that never occurs elsewhere in the New Testament (χωρὶς θεοῦ) or one that occurs over twenty times (χάριτι θεοῦ)? Is he likely to produce a statement that is bizarre and troubling or one that is familiar and easy?[9]

---

5. Lane, *Hebrews 1–8*, 43.
6. For a description see Metzger and Ehrman, *Text of the New Testament*, 91.
7. Ehrman, *Orthodox Corruption*, 146.
8. Zuntz, *Text of the Epistles*, 69.
9. Ehrman, *Orthodox Corruption*, 147.

Any theory of accidental corruption due to scribal carelessness would favor the less-attested reading, "apart from God" as the original. But some have argued that the change at Heb 2:9 was not accidental but intentional. In a long note on this verse in his eighth edition of the Greek New Testament (1872) Tischendorf suggested that "apart from God" (χωρὶς θεοῦ) was added in the margin to clarify the words of 2:8, "he left nothing that is not subject to him." The scribe, it is suggested, would have remembered 1 Cor 15:27b, "It is plain that this does not include the one who put all things in subjection under him." Both passages quote Ps 8:6. So remembering Paul's discussion in 1 Cor 15, the scribe of Heb 2 would have written "apart from God," (χωρὶς θεοῦ) in the margin. Some subsequent scribe would then have replaced the phrase "by the grace of God" in verse 9 with this phrase from the margin.[10] F. F. Bruce believed that this was the best explanation for the rise of the variation,[11] but Ehrman is probably right to conclude that this explanation is "altogether too clever, and requires too many dubious steps to work."[12] On the other hand, this explanation does alert us to the need to assess the textual question in 2:9 in its immediate context, and particularly to the quotation from Ps 8:5–7 (LXX) in Heb 2:6.

Ehrman's own proposal follows the suggestion of Tischendorf and others that the change was made from "apart from God" to "by the grace of God" for dogmatic reasons. He asserts that a proto-orthodox scribe, concerned that the reading "apart from God" would support the separationist view that the Christ separated from Jesus at his crucifixion, leaving him to die forsaken by God. He, or she, therefore changed the text to "by the grace of God" to avoid this construal. For Ehrman this was a clear example of "anti-separationist corruption" of scripture.[13]

## INTERNAL CRITERIA

In judgments on textual critical questions it is important to give due consideration to the style and theology of the author. In the case of Heb 2:9 it is especially helpful to do so. It is to be observed that "apart from" (χωρὶς) is used more often in Hebrews than in any other book of the

---

10. Tasker, "Text of the 'Corpus Paulinum,'" 184.
11. Bruce, *Hebrews*, 32. See also Attridge, *Hebrews*, 77.
12. Ehrman, *Orthodox Corruption*, 148.
13. Ibid., 146–50.

New Testament, whereas the word "grace" (χάρις) is never used in its several occurrences in Hebrews in reference to Christ's death for sin. Furthermore, J. K. Elliott has studied the use of χωρὶς in the epistle and has observed that it is always followed by an anarthrous noun (without an article) as it is here. On the other hand, grace (χάρις) is both preceded and followed by an article in the one true parallel (12:15).[14] So the stylistic as well as transcriptional considerations favor "apart from God" (χωρὶς θεοῦ) as the original reading at Heb 2:9.

## NARRATIVE CRITICAL STUDY

Ehrman has an intriguing note in his discussion of this variation. He writes, "It is at least conceivable that the author has Psalm 22 specifically in mind: 'My God, My God, why have you forsaken me?' It should not be overlooked that he does cite the psalm explicitly in the immediate context (v. 12)."[15] In the same year that Ehrman published his landmark study Paul Ellingworth brought out his large commentary on Hebrews. Ellingworth accepts χωρὶς θεοῦ (apart from God) "with some hesitation," and comments:

> The words allude to the desolation of Christ on the cross (Mk. 15:34 = Ps 22:1). In favor of this it may be said that Heb. 2:12 quotes Ps 22:22, and there are indications of the author's interest in the psalm as a whole.[16]

Both Ehrman and Ellingworth have hit on a clue that not only illumines the textual question but sheds fresh light on the whole passage: the importance of Psalm 22 for the story of Jesus that Hebrews is narrating.

Psalm 22[17] is one of the Old Testament passages that C. H. Dodd isolated as especially fruitful for early Christian testimonia, Old Testament passages that especially bore witness to Christ. No less than ten of its verses are cited in the New Testament.[18] Among expressions from Psalm 22 "quoted or echoed in the New Testament," Dodd includes two in Hebrews: "I will declare thy name . . ." (Ps 22:22 = Heb 2:12), "When

---

14. Elliott, "When Jesus," 339–41.
15. Ehrman, *Orthodox Corruption*, 176 n. 143.
16. Ellingworth, *Hebrews*, 156.
17. Note that the numbering of the Greek Psalms is different from the Hebrew, so that Psalm 22 in Hebrew is Psalm 21 in Greek.
18. Dodd, *According to the Scriptures*, 97.

he cried unto him he heard" (Ps 22:24 = Heb 5:7). If χωρὶς θεοῦ is what the author of Hebrews originally wrote, then we have a clear allusion to Ps 22:1, "My God, My God, why have you forsaken me?" This would constitute three references to Psalm 22 in the early chapters of Hebrews, indicating that the Psalm may have had an important influence in the shaping of the letter.

Dodd had argued that a number of frequently cited Old Testament passages constituted not just an "anthology of single, isolated prooftexts,"[19] but that whole passages were in view. These passages provided what Dodd called in his subtitle, "the Sub-Structure of New Testament Theology." Richard Hays carried Dodd's proposal a step further. In his *Echoes of Scripture in the Letters of Paul*, Hays studied the phenomenon of *intertextuality*, the imbedding of fragments of an earlier text within a later one. What Hays wrote of Paul could also be said of the other New Testament writers:

> The vocabulary and cadences of scripture—particularly of the LXX—are imprinted deeply in Paul's mind, and the great stories of Israel continue to serve for him as a fund of symbols and metaphors that condition his perceptions of the world, of God's promised deliverance of his people, and of his own identity and calling. His faith, in short, is one whose articulation is inevitably intertextual in character, and Israel's Scripture is the "determinate subtext that plays a constitutive role" in shaping his literary production.[20]

Hays' project has done much to awaken students of the New Testament to that fact that for Paul and the other New Testament writers scripture was not so much plundered as pondered. They treated the Old Testament as "a coherent story, not merely a grab-bag of isolated oracles."[21] In his own research on Rom 3, for example, Hays has demonstrated that Paul is not just quoting the language of Ps 143:2 (LXX 142) in Rom 3:20, but the logic of the whole psalm has shaped the argument. Paul here is not merely quoting a verse, but telling the story of the Psalm, which is a testimony to the righteousness of God.[22] Similarly, when Paul quotes Hab 2:4 in Rom 1:17, it is likely that he is not simply citing an iso-

---

19. Ibid., 59.
20. Hays, *Echoes*, 16, citing Greene, *The Light*, 50.
21. Hays, *Conversion*, 48.
22. Ibid., 50–60.

lated text to make his point about faith, but evoking the whole passage, Hab 1:1—2:4, which asserts the righteousness of God, even in the face of the contrary evidence of the invading Chaldeans. Perhaps no section of scripture has exercised a more notable shaping influence in the Pauline letters than Isaiah 40-55. Hays counts forty quotations and allusions in all.[23] Joel Marcus has conducted a similar study of the influence of this section on the synoptic tradition.[24] "The explicit citations are merely the tip of the iceberg," writes Hays, "They point to a larger mass just under the surface."[25]

Any reader of Hebrews will immediately be aware of the importance of the Old Testament in the letter. Modern studies have further refined the role of the Old Testament in Hebrews. In the eighteenth century J. A. Bengel called attention to the importance of certain Old Testament passages in the development of the argument in Hebrews, especially Psalms 2, 8 and 110. He pointed out that the introduction of a quotation from the Old Testament provided a point of departure for the argument that followed. Thus the Old Testament quotations in Hebrews are "functionally pivotal to the thematic development of the discourse."[26] In the twentieth century G. B. Caird proposed that the writer's argument is arranged in sections around four Old Testament texts: Ps 110:1-4; Ps 8:4-6; Ps 95:7-11; and Jer 31:31-34.[27] Others have added further refinement to Caird's thesis. For example J. Walters, in an unpublished paper entitled "The Rhetorical Arrangement of Hebrews," proposed that Hab 2:3-4 and Prov 3:11-12 should be added to Caird's list, and G. H. Guthrie insists that "an appreciation of the thematic development of the homily, the form of certain segments, and the transition between sections will often be dependent upon an understanding of the function of the OT texts in defining the arrangement and argument in Hebrews."[28]

Given these developments, a fresh study of the function of Psalm 22 in Hebrews is warranted. C. H. Dodd had proposed that there is one quotation (2:12) and one echo (5:7) of the Psalm. If the writer originally

---

23. Ibid., 38. On p. 39 Hays reproduces a chart drawn up by Diana Swancutt, illustrating vividly the impact of Isaiah 40-55 on Romans. See also Wagner, *Heralds*.

24. Marcus, *Way of the Lord*.

25. Hays, *Conversion*, 27.

26. Bengel, *Gnomon of the New Testament*, quoted in Lane, *Hebrews 1-8*, cxiii.

27. Caird, "Exegetical Method," 44-51.

28. Lane, *Hebrews 1-8*, cxv, who summarizes the researches of Walters and Guthrie.

wrote "apart from God" (χωρὶς θεοῦ) at 2:9, we have a third reference to the psalm in the early chapters of the letter. This may be but the "tip of the iceberg," to use Hays' expression. A good case may be made that Psalm 22 played a "constitutive role" in the letter. That the writer had Ps 22:1 clearly in mind is supported by the following considerations.

### The Speaker of Psalm 22

In Heb 2:10–12 there is a formula quotation from Ps 22:22:

> 10. It was fitting that God, for whom and through whom all things exist, in bringing many children to glory, should make the pioneer of their salvation perfect through sufferings. 11. For the one who sanctifies and those who are sanctified all have one Father. For this reason Jesus is not ashamed to call them brothers and sisters, 12. saying: I will proclaim your name to my brothers and sisters, in the midst of the congregation I will praise you.

The quotation from Psalm 22, together with the citations from Isa 8:17–18 in the verse that follows are both placed on the lips of Jesus. This phenomenon of Christ being the speaker of an Old Testament citation is a convention shared by other writers of the New Testament. In a perceptive essay entitled "Christ Prays the Psalms," Richard Hays notes several instances where Jesus is the voice praying the Old Testament:

To begin with, we note the voice of the pre-incarnate Christ praying the words of Psalm 40 in Heb 10:5–7:

> Sacrifices and offerings you have not desired,
> but a body you have prepared for me;
> in burnt offerings and sin offerings you have taken no pleasure.
> Then I said, "See, God, I have come to do your will, O God
> (in the scroll of the book it is written of me)."

In Rom 15:3 Christ prays the words of Ps 69:9: "The insults of those who insult you have fallen on me." This is followed in the same passage by a quotation from Ps 18:49: "Therefore I will confess you among the Gentiles, and sing praises to your name." John also knows this convention. In John 2:17 the other half of Ps 69:9 is cited indicating that Jesus is the speaker: "Zeal for your house will eat me up." The "I thirst" of the Johannine passion narrative (John 19:28) also assumes this convention. In the passion narrative in Luke's gospel the words "Into thy hands I commit my spirit" (Luke 23:46) echo Ps 31:5. And in what Hays calls a "daring hermeneutical strategy," the dying Jesus utters the opening words of Psalm 22: "My God, My God, why have you forsaken me?" (Mark 15:34; Matt 27:46). Nor is this a complete list. Hays writes of this convention:

> This quick survey of familiar texts demonstrates how widespread was the hermeneutical convention of hearing Christ's voice in the Psalms: John, the Synoptics, and Hebrews all bear witness, independently of Paul and of one another, to this interpretive tradition. Furthermore, all of them presuppose this remarkable convention without comment or justification. . . . Evidently this exegetical strategy was embedded in Christian reading of the Scriptures from the earliest identifiable time.[29]

The cry of dereliction in the passion narrative gives Ps 22:1 in the first person singular, as in the Psalm (Matt 27:46; Mark 15:34). But in the same context expressions echoing Psalm 22 are found in the third person. Given this technique in other New Testament writers (first and third person together in the use of Psalm 22) it is not surprising to find it here in Heb (2:12; 5:7; 2:9).

## The Shape of Psalm 22

Psalm 22 (LXX 21) contains two sections. The first part is the complaint of one who suffers and is brought "into the dust of death"(vv. 1–21). The concluding verses are the praise of one whom God has heard and delivered (vv. 22–31). It is this section of praise that is "drawn into the open"[30] by the explicit quotation of v. 22 at Heb 2:12. But any Jewish reader (and perhaps some Gentiles as well) would have heard the whole psalm. Hebrews is using here a literary technique, common in other New Testament writers, and traceable as far back as the first century writer Quintilian, called *transumption* or *metalepsis*. Hays describes *metalepsis* in the following way: "When a literary echo links the text in which it occurs to an earlier text, the figurative effect of the echo can lie in the unstated (transumed) points of resonance between the two texts."[31] Stated another way, Hays writes, "Paul's O.T. allusions and echoes frequently exemplify the literary trope of metalepsis. Metalepsis is a rhetorical and

29. Hays, *Conversion*, 107.
30. Ibid., 106.
31. Hays, *Echoes*, 20. Hays depends on the work of John Hollander, *The Figure of Echo*, See especially pp. 133–49.

poetic device in which the text alludes to an earlier text in a way that evokes resonances *beyond those explicitly cited.*"[32]

I am arguing that Hebrews no less than Paul exemplifies the literary trope of *metalepsis,* and that the reference to Psalm 22 is far more extensive than the quoted material in 2:12. This is, first of all, suggested by the *shape* of the psalm, which is divided into two distinct parts: the one about humiliation, the other about exaltation. This theme of humiliation and exaltation is also the theme of Hebrews 2. Another concern in Hebrews 2 is the unity of Christ and his "brothers and sisters," which is the main point of the quotation from Ps 22:22. It is significant that the shape of the psalm moves from a single figure, God-forsaken and pursued by enemies, to a leader of the congregation (22:26; "the great congregation"). This movement of the psalmist from lone complaint to community praise is also evident in other psalms of the righteous sufferer, especially 69. Moreover, it is interesting that the context of the following quotation from Isa 8:16–18 is linked in another way with Psalm 22:

> 16. Bind up the testimony, seal the teaching among my disciples.
> 17. I will wait for the Lord, who is hiding his face from the house of Jacob, and I will hope in him. 18. See, I and the children whom God has given me are signs and portents in Israel from the Lord of Hosts, who dwells on Mount Zion.

In verse 17 we read of God "hiding his face" from the house of Jacob. A theme echoed in the great deliverance of Ps 21:25 LXX:

> He did not despise or scorn the petition of the poor,
> nor did he turn away his face from me,
> but listened to me when I cried to him.[33]

It is possible, and likely, that the concern of the Lord "hiding his face" drew the two passages together in early Christian exegesis, as much as the solidarity of Jesus with his brothers and sisters. It is also likely that the link was made prior to the combined quotation in Hebrews.

There is one further observation on the trope of *metalepsis* and the shape of Psalm 22. In Ps 21:25 we read "nor did he turn his face from me, but listened to me when I cried to him." The idea of the Lord *listening* is a key to understanding the narrative of the psalm. The LXX of verse

32. Hays, *Conversion,* 2.
33. The translation is from Pietersma, *NETS.*

3 reads: "I cry by day but you will not listen." In the praise for the great deliverance the psalmist leads the congregation because "he listened to me when I cried to him" (verse 25). The theme of God not listening/listening provides an *inclusio* for the story the psalmist is telling. Many commentators have noticed an echo of these words in Heb 5:7:

> In the days of his flesh, Jesus offered up prayers and supplications, with loud cries and tears, to the one who was able to save him from death, and he was heard because of his reverent submission.[34]

These observations support the proposal that Ps 22:22 at Heb 2:12 is not an isolated proof-text, but rather "the tip of the iceberg" pointing to a larger mass of material beneath the surface. Hebrews no less than Paul is practiced at the use of the trope of *metalepsis*. Furthermore, it is apparent that not only the language but also the logic of Psalm 22 plays a constitutive role in Hebrews 2.

### *The Story of Psalm 22*

Psalm 22 tells the story of the righteous sufferer, his humiliation and exaltation. Humiliation and exaltation is also the story of Hebrews 2. It is reasonable, therefore, to conclude that Psalms 22 played a constitutive role in the shaping of Hebrews 2. Both the language and ideas of the psalm shaped the thought of this section of the letter. The story of the righteous sufferer, the story of his humiliation and exaltation exercised a formative influence on the earliest Christian community. At the end of his essay, "Christ Prays the Psalms," Richard Hays observes, "The interpretation of Jesus' death and resurrection, as far back as we can trace it, grows organically out of the matrix of the psalms of the righteous sufferer . . . Scripture, especially the Psalms, provides the matrix out of which early Christology grew."[35]

The psalms also provide the major Old Testament texts that shape the argument in Hebrews 2. Hebrews 2:6–8 cites Ps 8:4–6, and offers midrashic comment on the text in the subsequent verses:

---

34. We note that Harnack, followed by Bultmann, εὐλαβής, κτλ, *TDNT* 2, 753, proposes the conjecture "he was not heard" adding οὐκ before εἰσακουσθείς. This interpretation shows how tone-deaf some scholars can be to inter-testamental echoes.

35. Hays, *Conversion*, 118.

> When I look at your heavens,
> the work of your fingers,
> the moon and the stars that you have established;
> what are human beings that you
> Are mindful of them,
> mortals that you care for them?
> Yet you made them a little lower than God,
> and crowned them with glory and honor.
> You have given them dominion
> over the works of your hands;
> you have put all things under their feet.

The differences between the NRSV of Psalm 8 and the version of it quoted in Heb 2:6–8 are instructive. The writer to the Hebrews is dependent on the LXX and reads as follows:

> What are human beings that you are mindful of them,
> or mortals that you care for them?
> You have made them for a little while lower than the angels;
> you have crowned them with glory and honor,
> subjecting all things under their feet.

The NRSV casts both Old and New Testament statements in the plural, partly in the interest of "inclusive language," but both are singular in the original. Space dictates that we can only note two very interesting textual variations in Hebrews, both of which deserve careful consideration: instead of "what" a number of manuscripts read "who" (τίς); and a number of manuscripts add the missing line from the Hebrew and LXX, "and set him over the works of your hands." The interpreter must also navigate past the interpretations that see a developed "Son of Man" Christology (unlikely) or of a Gnostic or Hermetic background (less likely still)[36] and focus on how the Psalm functions in the argument of Hebrews.

Psalm 8:4–6 is interpreted by the writer of Hebrews to tell the story of how Jesus, the "man" of the psalm, has undergone "the suffering of death" in order that he might "taste death for all people" and how he is now "crowned with glory and honor." This is brought out by the writer's interpretation "a little lower than the angels." He turns the spatial reference of the psalm into a temporal one. Now Jesus is "for a little while" made lower than the angels. The story that is being told by Psalm 8, according to Hebrews, is the story of the humiliation and exaltation of

---

36. For a helpful discussion of these proposals see Attridge, *Hebrews*, 74.

humanity, fulfilled in Jesus. As Lane writes, "His experience of humiliation and exaltation guarantees that the absolute subjection of everything in Ps 8:7 and promised in Ps 110:1 will yet be achieved."[37]

It is clear, then, that for Hebrews both Psalm 8 and Psalm 22 tell the same story, the story of humiliation and exaltation. In Hebrews 2, Psalm 8 is the primary text and Psalm 22 is the secondary. Psalm 8 is the foregrounded text and Psalm 22 is in the background, the transumed text. But both converge to tell the same story: the story of the humiliation and exaltation of Jesus. That this is the story of Psalm 8 needs some explication and explanation, and is achieved in part by interpreting "a little lower" (βραχύτι) to mean "for a little while," and by the explicit mention of the name Jesus (for the first time in the epistle) only after the statement that he was for a little while made lower than the angels in verse 9. That the humiliation and exaltation of Jesus was the story of Psalm 22 for the early Christians needed no explanation. It was embedded in their thought and worship. Therefore Psalm 22 could be transumed by Hebrews, and remains beneath the surface until in 2:12, where it emerges as the dominant verse carrying forward the idea of Jesus' solidarity with his "brothers and sisters." The citation of Ps 22:22 in Heb 2:12 draws into the open the story of the whole psalm, which has been implied but not quoted to this point in the author's telling of the story of the humiliation and exaltation of Jesus. But Psalm 22 has not been wholly absent. I have argued that at 2:9, "apart from God," makes perfect sense when we consider the text in light of the story Hebrews is telling.

## TRANSMISSION HISTORY

The reading "apart from God" (χωρὶς θεοῦ), the less well attested reading at Heb 2:9, appears on internal and narrative grounds to be the original reading. It was probably replaced by an early copyist with the more familiar and less jarring "by the grace of God" (χάριτι θεοῦ). This may well have occurred because of the similarity of the two words. Faced with the choice of reading most copyists would have chosen the reading represented in the majority of our manuscripts. It is also likely that copyists who did not hear the echo of Ps 22:1 in 2:9 or recognize the importance of Psalm 22 for the early chapters of Hebrews would have failed to rec-

---

37. Lane, *Hebrews 1–8*, 48. So Attridge, *Hebrews*, 73, who notes that phrases drawn from the psalm, "understood as references to humiliation and exaltation, frame the name Jesus."

ognize the literary and theological value of the harder reading. Thus the modern editions and translations offer us a reading, true though it is to other New Testament teaching, that is less penetrating and less interesting than the more difficult reading "apart from God" (χωρὶς θεοῦ).

# 4

## Mark 15:34

IN THE PREVIOUS CHAPTER we considered the textual variation in Heb 2:9, advancing the suggestion that the variant reading "apart from God" is an echo of Ps 22:1. "My God, My God, why have you forsaken me?" This chapter will examine a textual variation in Mark 15:34, where this Psalm verse is quoted by Jesus as he is dying on the cross. In most of the manuscripts of Mark the reading follows this Psalm text and the parallel in Matt 27:46. But in Mark Codex D (Bezae) and several old Latin witnesses, as well as Porphyry have the striking reading "why have you reproached me?"

This variant reading, rejected by most commentators, and even ignored by some, has received fresh attention in recent years. Bart Ehrman argues that the reading "why have you forsaken me?" would have become very useful to the separationist Gnostics (who argued that the Christ came upon Jesus at his baptism and left him at his crucifixion) and that the proto-orthodox teachers and scribes of the second and third centuries would have found this teaching offensive. So some scribes would have been tempted to avoid the reading in Mark (the gospel preferred by the separationists, according to Irenaeus)[1] and so would have made the change from "forsaken me" (ἐγκατέλιπές με) to "reproached me" (ὠνείδισάς με).[2] In this chapter I will argue that *reproached me* (ὠνείδισάς με) is what Mark originally wrote. Admittedly, this will be a hard sell, but considered in light of the context of Mark, and of that writer's theological and literary art, it makes perfect sense, and is a pointer to Mark's ability as a storyteller. This is a far more satisfactory solution to the textual problem at Mark 15:34 than the suggestion of discomfort,

---

1. Irenaeus, *Against Heresies*, III.11.7.
2. Ehrman, *Orthodox Corruption*, 143–45; *Misquoting Jesus*, 172–73.

embarrassment, and corruption at the hands of a late second century proto-orthodox scribe.

## MANUSCRIPT SUPPORT

Bart Ehrman writes that the argument for "forsaken me" (ἐγκατέλιπές με) "is clinched by the overwhelmingly superior external attestation."[3] He notes that this reading is found in every Greek manuscript with the sole exception of Codex Bezae. It is found in all branches of the manuscript tradition, and is the form known to early Christian writers. But it is noteworthy that Ehrman advances this argument in support of the reading. On other occasions, when he defends as original readings with as slender support among the manuscripts, he avoids arguments about the oldest, best, most witnesses. Indeed, at Mark 1:41, where he defends the reading "becoming angry," rather than the better attested "moved with compassion," The same single Greek Manuscript (D) and a few old Latins support the reading. In that context Ehrman writes, "We are never completely safe in saying that when the vast majority of manuscripts have one reading and only a couple have the other, the majority are right. Sometimes a few manuscripts appear to be right even when all the others disagree."[4] I believe this to be the case at Mark 15:34.

Among modern scholars, Adolf von Harnack championed the reading "reproached me" as original, despite its slender manuscript support. Harnack argued that when Mark took over the translation (LXX) of the cry of derelication, which he had given in Aramaic, he changed "forsaken" to "reproached" in line with his narrative in which everyone else reproached Jesus. Now even God has reproached him. When Matthew used Mark as his source for the passion narrative, he used the Greek Old Testament reading. Subsequently scribes of Mark conformed their text either to Matthew or to the LXX.[5]

Ehrman noted that Harnack's argument, for all its ingenuity, has "done little to create for it a following."[6] This is not entirely true. Two important British scholars in the early twentieth century, F. C. Burkitt and C. H. Turner, believed that "reproached me" (ὠνείδισάς με) was

---

3. Ehrman, *Orthodox Corruption*, 145.
4. Ehrman, *Misquoting Jesus*, 134.
5. von Harnack, "Probleme," 86–104.
6. Ehrman, *Orthodox Corruption*, 145.

what Mark originally wrote in 15:34. Here is Burkitt's own story, written in 1900, of how he discovered unnoticed manuscript evidence for the reading:

> Cod. Bobiensis (k) is so well edited in *Old Latin Biblical Texts*, vol. ii, that the study of the MS itself might seem almost superfluous. Nevertheless in passing through Turin last October I took the opportunity of seeing *k*, and was fortunate enough to discipher one very important word where a later correction has almost effaced the original reading. In Mc. xv 34 *k* has . . . *ad quid me maledixisti* . . . The effect of the newly recovered reading is greatly to strengthen the case for ὠνείδισάς με (taunted me).[7]

Codex *k* is a fascinating manuscript with a second century text and an Irish connection. It was housed for most of its life in the monastery at Bobbio in Italy, and is believed to have been brought there by Columban, (d. 615) an early Irish missionary, and founder of that monastery.[8] William Sanday has demonstrated that its text agrees almost entirely with that of the African bishop Cyprian (c. 250) and therefore represents the text used in that part of the empire in the late second or early third century.[9] Its text at Mark 15:34 differs from the other two (European) Latin manuscripts that translate the Greek "reproached me" (ὠνείδισάς με). Here is Burkitt's tabulation:

| | |
|---|---|
| Me maledixisti | *k* (fourth century) |
| Exprobrasti me | *c* (eleventh-twelfth century) |
| Me in opprobrium dedisti | *i* (fifth-sixth century) |

Here are three independent attempts, one from North Africa and two from Europe, to translate the striking Greek variant. The geographical spread of the reading is further widened by its appearance in the Harclean Syriac version (Sy[h]) and in the third century anti-Christian writer Porphyry. The manuscript support is not quite so meager as is often assumed.

---

7. Burkitt, *JTS* I (1900) 278–79.

8. For details see Metzger, *Early Versions*, 315–16. Metzger notes especially the variant at Mark 15:34.

9. Wordsworth, Sanday, and White, *Old Latin Biblical Texts, No. II.*

## TRANSCRIPTIONAL PROBABILITIES

C. H. Turner wrote concerning the variant "reproached me" (ὠνείδισάς με) "As no one could have thought of inventing this reading, it must certainly be accepted as what Mark wrote."[10] Ehrman has now suggested a reason for inventing the reading. What, then are the transcriptional probabilities?

"Reproached me" (ὠνείδισάς με) is certainly the more difficult reading, and where scribes found it, the temptation would be great to harmonize it either to Matthew, the most popular gospel in the early church, or to Psalm 22 (21 LXX), a psalm embedded in its worship and theology. Another reason for the substitution of "forsaken me" (ἐγκατέλιπές με) for the more difficult reading was a perceived mistranslation of the Hebrew or Aramaic. A related issue is whether Mark or Matthew gave the citation in Hebrew or in Aramaic. On this matter commentators have been divided. Indeed all the variants in Mark 15:34/ Matt 27:46 need to be considered together and interface with one another. What word did Mark or Matthew use for "why" (εἰς τί or ἱνατί)? Is the verb "forsaken/reproached" the last word in the sentence, or is it "me"? Finally, was Mark, upon whom Matthew depends, giving a translation of the Hebrew or Aramaic form or an interpretation?[11]

## INTERNAL CRITERIA

The reading *reproached me* (ὠνείδισάς με) is consistant with both the theme and vocabulary of Mark. Indeed the word is used just two verses earlier (15:32): "Those who were crucified with him reproached him" (καὶ οἱ συνεσταυρωμένοι σὺν αὐτῷ ὠνείδιζον αὐτόν). Harnack argued that the use of the more difficult reading in Mark 15:34 conforms to Mark's passion story in which *everyone* reproaches or mocks the silent Jesus. Now he cries that even God has reproached him.[12] But the key to understanding Mark's peculiar reading in 15:34 is not only in its suitability to his passion narrative, but in his creative interpretation of the two Psalm texts he understands especially to have found fulfillment in the crucifixion of Jesus: Psalm 22 and Psalm 69.

---

10. Turner, *St. Mark*, 79.

11. Manson, "The Old Testament,"312–32. See also the valuable discussion of these related textual issues in Stendahl, *The School of Matthew*, 83–87.

12. von Harnack, "Probleme" 1:86–104, Ehrman, *Orthodox Corruption*, 173.

## NARRATIVE CONSIDERATIONS

Both Psalm 22 and Psalm 69 are quoted or echoed several times in Mark's passion narrative. The United Bible Societies fourth edition of the Greek New Testament gives the following parallels:

```
Mark 15:24 = Ps 22:18
Mark 15:29 = Ps 22:7
Mark 15:34 = Ps 22:1
Mark 15:23 = Ps 69:21
Mark 15:36 = Ps 69:21
```

These two Psalms are part of a larger group, labeled by H. Gunkel in the form-critical category "laments of an individual,"[13] and are generally referred to in contemporary scholarship as "the Psalms of the Righteous Sufferer."[14] Echoes of other Psalms of this group have been detected in Mark's passion narrative (35, 38, 41). But recent study has focuses on 22 and 69 as the primary texts that influenced Mark 15. James Edwards asserts that Psalms 22 and 69 "reverberate throughout the passion narrative" in Mark.[15] For at least these two Psalms of the Righteous Sufferer it is likely that in Mark 15 the cited material is only the tip of the iceberg, revealing a larger mass underneath.[16] Although only a few words are echoed at any given point, writer and readers would recognize the whole of the psalm being evoked by the words. Thus the *story* of Palms 22 or 69 would be present to those who heard Mark's passion narrative.[17]

Whereas several verses of Psalm 22 are echoed in Mark 15 only Ps 69:21 can be clearly detected as an influence on this passion narrative. Nevertheless, the fact that other phrases from Psalm 69[18] are important testimonia for early Christianity (John 2:17 and Rom 15:3 cite the two halves of Ps 69:10) and that Matthew and John both cite Ps 69:21 as fulfilled in the passion of Jesus further strengthens the likelihood that the whole Psalm was in view in Mark.[19]

---

13. Gunkel, *Die Psalmen*.

14. Marcus, *Way of the Lord*, 172. For a full discussion of these psalms in the passion narratives see Moo, *Old Testament*, 225–300. Moo gives a comprehensive chart of OT citations in the passion narratives in 285–86.

15. Edwards, *Mark*, 476.

16. Hays, *Conversion*, 27.

17. Carey, *Cry*, passim.

18. Dodd, *According to the Scriptures*, 57–60.

19. See also the citation of Ps 69:25 in Acts 1:20, concerning the filling of the vacancy caused by the betrayal and death of Judas.

I am arguing that the words "reproached me" (ὠνείδισάς με) at Mark 15:34 were what Mark originally wrote. This is suggested by the observation that the word "reproach" (ὀνειδίζω etc.) is a key word, perhaps *the* key word, in Psalm 68 (LXX).

The word recurs in Psalm 68 (LXX) in verses 7, 9 (twice), 10, 19, and 20. According to Mark (as Ehrman has noted) everyone reproaches Jesus in his crucifixion. Now Mark adds that God has not only abandoned Jesus but reproached him. Mark achieves this by changing the last word of the quotation from Ps 22:1 (21:1 LXX) to the unspoken keyword of Psalm 69. Psalm 22 has been the primary text in Mark 15, Psalm 69 the secondary one. But the keyword from Psalm 69 surfaces in its combination with Ps 22:1. In this way Mark teaches that on the cross Jesus was both forsaken by God, and suffered the reproach of God. His teaching is thus not dissimilar to the thought of Paul in Gal 3:13 (quoting Deut. 21:23): "Cursed is everyone who hangs on a tree."[20]

Another reason for thinking that "reproached me" (ὠνείδισάς με) is what Mark wrote in 15:34 is that if the word "reproach" (ὀνειδίζω) has been drawn from Psalm 68 (LXX) the citation conforms to a feature which we may observe elsewhere in Mark: his creative melding of two or more phrases from different Old Testament passages. We have already seen this technique at work in the voice at the baptism (Mark 1:11) where Mark combines phrases from Ps 2:7, Isa 42:1, and Gen 22:1. The same citation/interpretation technique is also found in Mark 14:62, where "Jesus answers the high priest's question about his identity with a response that melds a quotation from Daniel with an allusion to Psalm 110."[21]

> Again the high priest asked him, "Are you the Messiah the
> Son of the Blessed One?" Jesus said, "I am; and
> 'you will see the Son of Man seated at the right hand of the Power'
> and 'coming with the clouds of heaven.'"

The allusive combination of phrases from Dan 7 and Isa 53 has been detected by many commentators at Mark 10:45:

> For the Son of Man came not to be served but to serve,
> and to give his life a ransom for many.

---

20. I am grateful to Richard Hays for drawing this parallel to my attention in 1987.
21. Marcus, *Way of the Lord*, 1.

This same technique, of melding phrases from two or more Old Testament passages, may also be detected in Mark's words of institution of the Lord's supper, in the words concerning the cup (Mark 14:23-25). The Nestle-Aland 27 text notes several Old Testament Echoes (Exod 24:8; Zech 9:11; Jer 31: 31-34; Isa 53:11).

> Then he took a cup, and after giving thanks he gave it to them, and all of them drank from it. He said to them, "This is my blood of the covenant, which is poured out for many. Truly I tell you, I will never again drink of the fruit of the vine until that day when I drink it new in the kingdom of God."[22]

We also note the combination of Mal 3:1; Isa 40:3; and Exod 23:20 in Mark 2:1-3. These three texts are introduced as "written in the prophet Isaiah," a formula changed by later scribes to "in the Prophets." Mark's melding technique may provide a clue to his introductory formula, misunderstood by later copyists, but focusing on the dominant text in the combination from Isaiah 40.

This technique, which we may call "composite echo," was fully explored by H. C. Kee, who noted similarities with scripture exegesis at Qumran. Kee wrote:

> The most significant parallel between Markan exegesis and the exegetical method employed at Qumran is the juxtaposition of scriptures that in their origins had little or nothing to do with each other, but which in the hands of the exegete are shown to be mutually illuminating and to give rise to theological perceptions that were not anticipated in any of the original components and that thus define the eschatological community, its hopes and obligations.[23]

Kee cites the following composite echoes in Mark. (Some of these are formula quotations, where the combination technique is assumed, but not stated, and would be recognized in most cases by writer and reader alike):

---

22. Here we note the NRSV translation of the UBS[4]/ NA[27] text, but must recognize the textual variations in the words of institution in the synoptics and in 1 Cor 11:23-25, each of which must be considered on its own merits.

23. Kee, "The Function," 181.

| | |
|---|---|
| Mark 1:2–3 | (Exod 23:20/Mal 3:1/Isa 40:3) |
| Mark 1:11 | (Isa 42:1/Ps 2:7)[24] |
| Mark 11:1–11 | (Zech 9:9/Ps 118:25–6) (Isa 56:7/Jer 7:11)[25] |
| Mark 12:1–12 | (Isa 5:1–2/Ps 118:22–23) |
| Mark 13:24–26 | (Isa 34:4/Josh 2:10/Ezek 32:7–8/Dan 7:13–14) |
| Mark 14:62 | (Dan 7:13/Ps 110:1) |

This is not an exhaustive list, and I argue here that Mark 15:34 should be added to it. I sum up, then, the argument for considering "reproached me" (ὠνείδισάς με) as the original reading at Mark 15:34. Although the manuscript attestation is not as strong as that for the printed reading, the few witnesses that support it are important ones. Moreover "reproached me" (ὠνείδισάς με) is certainly the more difficult reading, and it is easy to see how its presence in the text of Mark might give rise to the change. The word "reproach" (ὀνειδίζω) is a key word in the LXX of Psalm 68, a psalm echoed in Mark's passion narrative. Finally, the conflation of two or more biblical texts as a "composite echo" is a "typical Marcan strategy."[26] So the combination of the key word from Psalm 69 with the leading verse from Psalm 22 in the cry of dereliction corresponds to Mark's literary achievements elsewhere in his gospel.

But if this combination is a literary achievement, it is also a theological achievement. Psalm 69 is used in Mark and elsewhere in the New Testament as a messianic testimonium. Barnabas Lindars argues that Psalm 69 is "demonstrably the most widely used psalm in the Passion apologetic" of the New Testament.[27] But any reader of this psalm will recognize a problem in seeing the whole of the psalm as applying to Jesus the Messiah. The beginning section, verses 1–22, depicts the righteous sufferer. The final section, verses 30–36, is a song of praise to the Lord who has heard the cry of the needy, and a promise that "God will save Zion and rebuild the cities of Judah." (v. 35). In between these sections, verses 23–29 record a series of jarring imprecations against enemies:

---

24. Note that Kee does not include Gen 22:1, 12, 16, which we would add to this composite echo.

25. Perrin, *Temple*, 84 notes that this combination indicates "a much longer homiletic iceberg originating with Jesus, and now hidden from the view of history"

26. Marcus, *Way of the Lord*, 54.

27. Lindars, *New Testament Apologetic*, 106.

> ²³ May their eyes be darkened so they cannot see,
> and their backs be bent forever.
> ²⁴ Pour out your wrath on them;
> let your fierce anger overtake them.
> ²⁵ May their place be deserted;
> let there be no one to dwell in their tents.
> ²⁶ For they persecute those you wound
> and talk about the pain of those you hurt.
> ²⁷ Charge them with crime upon crime;
> do not let them share in your salvation.
> ²⁸ May they be blotted out of the book of life
> and not be listed with the righteous.
> ²⁹ I am in pain and distress;
> may your salvation, O God, protect me.[28]

Lindars points out that almost every line of these imprecatory or cursing verses is quoted or alluded to in the New Testament.[29] But we notice that none of them is employed by Jesus or the gospel writers in the passion narratives. No better comment may be found on this phenomenon than 1 Pet 2:23: "When he was abused, he did not return abuse; when he suffered, he did not threaten." Furthermore, the combination of Psalm 69 with Psalm 22 affects a re-interpretation of the former. Psalm 22 contains no such cursing. Rather it is the complaint and the vivid description of the suffering righteous one, who is heard and delivered by God. By combining the two psalms as a composite echo, Mark disarms the imprecations of Psalm 69 by the non-cursing trust of the primary text, Psalm 22. But in the combination of the two psalms in Mark's passion narrative Psalm 69 has made a distinctive contribution. For Psalm 22 the enemies of the righteous reproach him. In Psalm 69:26 it is God who is reproaching the sufferer. Robert Alter's new translation of the Psalm brings this sense of God being the one reproaching to the fore: "And you . . . whom you struck they pursued."[30] Now it is God who is reproaching the righteous sufferer. Everyone else in the Markan passion narrative has reproached Jesus. Now in 15:34 God also reproaches him. Thus Jesus takes upon himself on the cross the reproach of both men and God. He absorbs it and disarms all the curse and punishment in his death. This teaching of Mark, implied by the alternate reading at 15:34, is

---

28. Psalm 69:23–29 NIV.
29. Lindars, *New Testament Apologetic*, 105.
30. Alter, *Psalms*, 240.

consistent with the story Mark is narrating with echoes of Psalm 22 and Psalm 69, and corresponds to teaching elsewhere in the New Testament (Gal 3:13).

## TRANSMISSION HISTORY

The preceding proposal suggests the following transmission history for Mark 15:34. In writing his gospel Mark changed Ps 22:1 in the cry of dereliction by replacing the word "forsaken" with the word "reproached," the key word from Psalm 69. Later scribes, not attuned to Mark's literary and theological art of combining words from different Old Testament texts, conformed the reading, either accidentally or intentionally, to the more familiar words of Ps 22:1 or Matt 27:46. This tendency in transmission explains why the more difficult reading, "reproached me" (ὠνείδισάς με) has survived in only a handful of witnesses.

# 5

# Luke 22:43–44

THE 139 LETTERS THAT comprise Luke 22:43–44 are printed in the UBS⁴/Nestle²⁷ edition of the Greek New Testament, enclosed in double brackets. This indicates that although they are printed in the text rather than in the margin, they are regarded as "later additions to the text, but which are of evident antiquity and importance."[1] Here UBS⁴ and its predecessor, UBS³, follow the practice of WH, but the first two editions of the UBS relegated the two verses to the margin, assigning a {C} rating to the decision of the committee. Most modern editors deem them to be a later addition, but some would include them in the text.[2] It is no surprise that commentators are divided as to whether these verses are original with Luke.[3] These circumstances invite a fresh study of these verses.

## MANUSCRIPT EVIDENCE

The chief manuscript evidence for omission and inclusion in Luke is as follows:

Omit: P⁶⁹ᵛⁱᵈ P⁷⁵ ℵ¹ B
Include: ℵ* ℵ² D

Fitzmyer notes, "The external witnesses to the text are almost equally divided, with what are usually considered the better Greek manuscripts

---

1. UBS⁴, 47*.
2. Kilpatrick, *Diglot: Luke* (London: BFBS, 1962), 68. Huck, Greeven, 245. Tischendorf 8th edition, with a long note.
3. Bock, *Luke*, 1764. See Clivaz, *L'Ange, passim.* For a comprehensive (733 pages!) review of the evidence and scholarship, which reaches the same conclusion as this chapter.

on the side of omitting the verses."[4] But the external considerations of a reading include not only papyri and majuscules, but also versions, lectionaries and patristic quotations. It is noteworthy that the longer reading is found in Justin Martyr, Irenaeus, Hippolytus, Eusebius, Didymus, and Jerome. This indicates clearly that the words were present in second century manuscripts of Luke. J. K. Elliott notes, "The words were controversial even at an early date and that they occasioned changes in both directions in one particular manuscript (א)."[5]

Any study of this variation must begin with the essay by F. J. A. Hort, who notes the complexity of the evidence in the minuscules, the lectionaries and the patristic quotations.[6] Hort judges the words to be a "Western interpolation, adapted in eclectic texts ... a fragment from traditions, written or oral, which were, for a while at least, locally current beside the canonical Gospels ... among the remains of this evangelic tradition which were rescued from oblivion by the scribes of the second century."[7] While this essay will take issue with Hort's conclusions, his appreciation of the complexities surrounding the manuscript evidence, not least their appearance in family 13 and several lectionaries after Matt 26:39, makes it clear that the question of their genuineness cannot be solved by the use of external (manuscript) criteria alone.

## INTERNAL CRITERIA

Luke 22:43–44 has been much discussed from the standpoint of its style and literary form. In particular, Bart Ehrman and Mark Plunkett have argued vigorously that the vocabulary of the verses are non-Lucan, and that their inclusion in the text interrupts the chiastic structure of the passage.[8] However, Raymond Brown studies the vocabulary of the verses carefully and concludes that "in style and vocabulary this passage is closer to Luke than to any other NT author."[9] Brown also challenges Ehrman and Plunkett's proposal concerning chiastic structure, which gives them "convincing reason for rejecting Lucan authorship." He judges this

4. Fitzmyer, *Luke*, 1443.
5. Elliott, "Thoroughgoing Eclecticism," 116–17.
6. Hort and Westcott, "Notes on Select Readings," 64–67.
7. Ibid., 66–67.
8. Ehrman and Plunkett, "The Angel," 401–16. Ehrman, *Orthodox Corruption*, 187–94.
9. Brown, *Death of the Messiah*, 182.

to be "another example of exaggerated chiasm," and cites others who have found chiastic structure that includes verses 43–44.[10] Arguments from style and structure appear to be as inconclusive as those from the external manuscript evidence in resolving the textual dilemma of this passage.

## TRANSCRIPTIONAL PROBABILITIES

F. J. A. Hort made a strong assertion in reviewing the evidence for Luke 22:43–44:

> Notwithstanding the random suggestions of rash or dishonest handling thrown out by controversialists there is no tangible evidence for the excision of a substantial portion of narrative for doctrinal reasons at any period of textual history. Moreover, except to heretical sects, which exercised no influence over the transmitted text, the language of vv. 43f. would be no stumbling block in the first and second centuries; and to a later time than this it would be impossible to refer the common original of the documents which attest omission.[11]

Bart Ehrman has offered a serious challenge to this assertion in his pioneering study, *The Orthodox Corruption of Scripture*. Ehrman claims that under the pressure of debates with Docetics, proto-orthodox Christian scribes would be tempted to add the words to the text of Luke's gospel, to emphasize the full humanity of Jesus.[12] Some have found this a plausible explanation of the textual variation.[13] Others, however, have argued that the verses were original and were removed by an early copyist who thought they "might supply comfort to those who challenged the divinity of Jesus."[14] Such a challenge to the orthodox position was made by Celsus (Origen, *Contra Celsum*, 2.24). John Nolland rightly concludes, "The arguments for and against inclusion are finely balanced. Both addition and removal are explicable in terms of arguments over Christology."[15]

---

10. Gamba, "Agonia," 159–66.
11. Hort and Westcott, *The New Testament*," 2:66.
12. Ehrman, *Orthodox Corruption*, 225–26. *Misquoting Jesus*, 139–44; 164–65.
13. Parker, *Living Text*, 157–59.
14. Brown, *Death of the Messiah*, 184
15. Nolland, *Luke*, 1080.

To sum up, then, plausible arguments for accepting and rejecting Luke 22:43–44 as original with Luke can be made on grounds of manuscript attestation, internal criteria, and transcriptional probabilities, and they cancel each other out. No final decision on the textual question can be made on the basis of these considerations. Another line of inquiry is called for.

## NARRATIVE FEATURES

Given the stalemate in the traditional areas of text-critical research, we must look elsewhere for further light on the textual question in Luke 22:43–44. Here we find some proposals that have been made concerning possible Old Testament allusions and broader narrative themes within the verses. In the *Commentary on the New Testament Use of the Old Testament* David Pao and Eckhard Schnabel note that some scholars have suggested that the scene has been "created from O.T. passages." The following are proposed: Job 42:2; Ps 89:9; Gen 3:19; Isa 53:3, 10; Ps 22:2,3,15; Isa 51:17,22; Jer 25:15,17, 28; Ezek 23:31-34; Zech 12:2; Ps 11:6-7; 1 Kgs 19:5-6; Dan 3:28.[16] Of all these proposals the one that seems to be most plausible is the reference to Isa 53, the fourth Isaianic Servant Song (Isa 52:13—53:12). In 1974 William Larkin argued that the figure of the Servant may provide the OT background.

> The Isaianic Servant of God who obediently suffers as he completes his divinely appointed destiny and in that suffering receives divine aid is the OT figure who best accounts for all the elements in this brief incident.[17]

That there was a unified concept of the Suffering Servant in the Second Temple period and that Jesus saw his mission in these terms has been challenged.[18] That Luke presented Jesus as understanding his death in terms of Isaiah 53 is undeniable, since he quotes 53:12 in Luke 22:37: "For I tell you, this scripture must be fulfilled in me, 'and he was counted with the lawless.'" In fact, Kim Haines-Eitzen notes, "Luke has a certain proclivity for Isaiah 53 and especially verse 12."[19] Haines-Eitzen's com-

---

16. Pao and Schnabel, "Luke," 389.
17. Larkin, "Background," 253.
18. Hooker, *Servant*. For recent discussion of the question see Bellinger and Farmer, *Suffering Servant*. Janowski and Stuhlmacher, *Suffereing Servant*.
19. Haines-Eitzen, *Guardians*, 121.

ment occurs in a discussion of Luke 23:34a, "Father, forgive them, for they do not know what they are doing." Although there are reasons to question her thesis that the words were removed by an early scribe due to anti-Judaic bias (following Ehrman),[20] her arguments regarding Isa 53:12 and the value of this allusion for establishing the text of this verse are pioneering.

Here also, at Luke 23:34, we have a verse in Luke's Gospel hotly debated by modern textual critics, and one in which the evidence for inclusion or omission is evenly balanced. Moreover, it is a saying that incorporates an allusion to Isa 53:12, "He made intercession for the transgressors." Haines-Eitzen's observation is important for our discussion of the similar variation at Luke 22:43–44, and for the other essays in this volume, because she has noted the value of quotations, allusions and echoes from the scriptures of Israel for establishing the New Testament text. With these verses, as on other occasions, we have noted that evidence for and against taking the words as original with a New Testament author is inconclusive. Additional material and perspective is needed if the question is to be resolved. The scriptural citations found in the disputed words may offer that additional piece of evidence.

The allusion to Isa 53:12 at Luke 23:34 is followed directly by a clear reference to Ps 22:18. The latter reference is secure in the textual tradition. These two passages, Isaiah 53 and Psalm 22 both had a formative influence on the passion narratives in the gospel tradition. They did not create the details of the narrative so much as give theological explanation for the details described by the evangelists. This juxtaposition of one Old Testament allusion on top of another is common in the New Testament, and is akin to both the catena method of citing scriptures (Romans 15, 1 Peter 2) and to the composite echoes of scripture (Mark 10:45; 14:62). A comparison of these various styles of combining different texts from the scriptures of Israel is called for, but would require another monograph.

What is important for our purpose in this study is to notice that the two scripture texts combined in Luke 23:34 (assuming the longer text is original) are among the texts of the OT most likely to form the background to the narrative in Luke 22:43–44: Isaiah 53 and Psalm 22.[21] These texts were of supreme importance for the New Testament

---

20. See Rodgers Review of Haines-Eitzen, 404–7.

21. Pao and Schnabel, *Commentary on the New Testament,* 389. Note that Justin, *Dialogue with Trypho,* links Luke 22:43–44 with a running commentary in Psalm 22.

writers as they sought to present the story of Jesus as the suffering and vindicated Messiah. It is therefore possible to see these verses in Luke 22 not as a later addition to Luke's gospel, but as another Lucan allusion to these two Old Testament passages which help him to explain the passion narrative elsewhere (Luke 22:37; 23:34b). The story of the suffering Messiah, according to the scriptures, is a key to the solution of the textual dilemma.

Recent study of the use of the Old Testament in the New Testament has emphasized the way in which the broader narrative thrust of a section of scripture has been appropriated by the New Testament writer. It is not just that one finds here and there a quotation or detects an allusion or echo from second Isaiah. Rather the *story* Isaiah is narrating has become the *story* of Jesus the Messiah. Several studies offer valuable examples of this approach. Joel Marcus, in his study, *The Way of the Lord*, demonstrated significant influence of the narrative of Isaiah on the Gospel of Mark.[22] Rikki E. Watts's influential study, *Isaiah's New Exodus in Mark*,[23] shows how the longed-for return from exile, proclaimed by Second Isaiah, is retold by Mark as fulfilled in the the coming, life, death and Resurrection of Jesus. Ross Wagner has offered a similar study of Romans, especially chapters 9–11 and 15. The whole of Isaiah, and especially chapters 51–55 have had a formative influence on Paul's thought.[24] These writers have shown that Mark and Paul did not treat the OT as a "grab bag of isolated oracles,"[25] but were steeped in the grand narrative of scripture and told it afresh in light of Jesus Christ.[26] And what was true of Mark and Paul may also be said of Luke. Indeed Luke's attention to the broader scriptural narrative has been studied with regard to Acts.[27] It would be surprising not to find the same attention to the story of Exodus/New Exodus in Luke's Gospel. When we turn to the Gospel of Luke we find, in fact, a special focus on Jesus as embodying the new Exodus. Nowhere is this seen more clearly than in Luke's addition to the Transfiguration story that Jesus spoke with Moses and Elijah about his "exodus" (ἔξοδον) which he was about to accomplish at Jerusalem"

22. Marcus, *Way of the Lord*.
23. Watts, *Isaiah's New Exodus*.
24. Wagner, *Heralds of the Good News*.
25. Hays, *Conversion*, 48.
26. Bauckham, "Reading Scripture," 38–53.
27. Pao, *Acts and the Isaianic New Exodus*.

(Luke 9:31). But like Mark, Luke also sees Jesus *Exodus* through the lens of Second Isaiah. In addition the special emphasis on Isaiah 53, noted by Haines-Eitzen, we observe the long citation from Isa 40:3–5 in Luke 3:44–46, quoting the passage more extensively than the other gospels. Note also Jesus' programmatic citation of Isa 61:1–2 in the synagogue at Nazareth, with his comment, "Today this scripture has been fulfilled in your hearing" (Luke 4:21).[28] Indeed, it is possible to talk of "Isaiah's New Exodus in Luke." In light of these observations, it is plausible that when Luke told the story of Jesus' agony in the garden he had in mind Isa 53:3, 12, from the passage he has just quoted (Luke 22:37) the passage, in the broader context of Isaiah, that provided the scriptural template for his theological reflection on Jesus death and resurrection. In the words of Brevard Childs, Luke saw "the morphological fit between Isaiah 53 and the passion of Jesus."[29]

## TRANSMISSION HISTORY

The conclusion regarding the textual question at Luke 22:43–44 suggested above was summed up by Streeter long ago, "B W 579 etc., which omit the words, though they may possibly give the earliest Alexandrian text, do not preserve the original words of Luke."[30]

How, then, shall we trace the transmission history of this longer variation in the Gospel of Luke. Written by Luke as an integral part of his passion narrative, the words would have been "heard" by their earliest readers as an echo of Isaiah 53, and of Psalm 22. In the second and third century church, increasingly gentile in composition, the echoes would have been less discernible. Other issues would clamor for attention. The possibility that scribes who were zealous to maintain a high picture of the divinity of Jesus would have removed them cannot be ruled out. Other scribes, then, not finding the words in their copies of Luke may well have wanted to insert them to assert the humanity of Jesus. Neither scenario is impossible, but both are unlikely among proto-orthodox scribes, whose leaders exhibited a scrupulous fidelity in copying the text they had received.[31] The possibility that the words could

---

28. Unlike modern interpreters, the earliest Christian writers did not distinguish between Isaiahs 1, 2, and 3. Nor did they isolate the servant songs from the whole book.

29. Childs, *Isaiah*, 423.

30. Streeter, *Four Gospels*, 138.

31. See Rodgers, review of Ehrman, *Misquoting Jesus*, 38–39.

have been omitted accidentally should also be considered. These are not mutually exclusive proposals, but all of these developments may have been operating in the course of transmission in the second and third centuries. Such complexity in the transmission history of the text makes the situation both confusing and exciting for the historian of the text.

# 6

## Acts 20:28

ONE OF THE BEST known and most discussed textual variations in the Acts of the Apostles is found in Acts 20:28:

> Keep watch over yourselves and over all the flock, of which the Holy Spirit has made you overseers, to shepherd the church of God, that he obtained with the blood of his own Son. (NRSV)

In this verse we find two textual variations which are related to each other. Our printed texts read "to shepherd the church of God" (ποιμαίνειν τὴν ἐκκλησίαν τοῦ θεοῦ). However, a number of manuscripts read "the church of the Lord" (ἐκκλησίαν τοῦ κυρίου). This variation is related to the one at the end of the verse, where Paul speaks of God (or the Lord) purchasing the church "with his own blood" (τοῦ αἵματος τοῦ ἰδίου). We will look at each of these variations separately, conscious that they are related.

### MANUSCRIPT AND STYLISTIC CONSIDERATIONS

For the reading "the church of God" there are actually seven readings, but only two merit serious consideration.[1] "The church of the Lord" is supported by P[74] A C* D etc. "The church of God" by ℵ B etc. Clearly the matter of the original reading cannot be decided on the basis of external manuscript evidence alone. When we turn to internal criteria, we find that a decision is not possible on grounds of style and usage as well. While the phrase "the church of God" occurs nowhere else in the New Testament, it is found seven times in the LXX. On the other hand, the expression "the church of the Lord" occurs eleven times in the Pauline corpus. This may point to the latter as a Pauline expression, but

---

1. Metzger and Ehrman, *Text of the New Testament*, 332.

caution must be exercised in pressing this argument. Neither external (manuscript) nor internal (style and usage) considerations can settle the matter. The RSV and NRSV have adopted "the church of God." NEB and REB have printed "the church of the Lord." Most scholars today would favor *the church of God,* and argue that it is the more difficult reading, especially in light of the rest of the verse which reads "the church of God that he purchased with his own blood." C. S. C. Williams notes in his commentary that later scribes would tend to substitute "Lord" for "God" to avoid Patripasian implications.[2]

The words of the second variation are translated by NRSV "with the blood of his own Son." However, we note that the equivalent of the word "Son" is not present in the Greek text (διὰ τοῦ αἵματος τοῦ ἰδίου). The reading is supported by ℵ A B C D, etc. and is preferred by modern editors to the Byzantine text (ἰδίου αἵματος), which is often found in the later manuscripts with the conflated reading, *the church of the Lord and God.*

## TRANSCRIPTIONAL PROBABILITIES

Most scholars today would follow the UBS[4]/NA[27] text "The church of God which he obtained with his own blood (or the blood of his own)" (τὴν ἐκκλησίαν τοῦ θεοῦ, ἣν περιεποιήσατο διὰ τοῦ αἵματος τοῦ ἰδίου.). To later copyists the suggestion that God shed blood would have caused difficulty, and the change to "the Lord" (τοῦ κυρίου) which could mean either God or Jesus, would alleviate the difficulty. The pressure of the debate with the Patripassionists (who taught that the father actually suffered in the crucifixion) could have added to the temptation to change. If we grant that this was the trajectory of textual change, we still need to ask why Luke would represent Paul as using the unusual expression of God obtaining the church with his own blood. At this point narrative considerations can help in demonstrating not only the appropriateness of the expression but also its richness.

## NARRATIVE FEATURES

A thorough critical study of Acts 20:28 will explore all the intertextual elements in the verse, within the context of Paul's speech to the Ephesian

---

2. Williams, *Acts,* 234. See also a fuller discussion in Ehrman, *Orthodox Corruption,* 87–88, 264.

elders (Acts 20:18–35). What elements of Israel's story lie beneath the surface of Paul's speech, and how readily would his audience have heard the echoes of scripture in this speech of Paul? We begin with the expression "with his own blood," or "with the blood of his own." Reviewing the textual difficulties of the verse, F. J. A. Hort had suggested that the word "Son" (υἱοῦ) actually stood in the original text of Acts and had fallen out in the course of transmission.[3] But F. F. Bruce dubbed Hort's suggestion an unnecessary conjecture in light of the technical meaning of τοῦ ἰδίου in early Christian parlance as referring to "his own dear son."[4] That technical meaning was noted by Metzger in the *Textual Commentary*, in his report of the UBS committee discussion of the textual issues in the verse. Metzger wrote:

> The absolute use of ὁ ἴδιος is found in Greek papyri as a term of endearment referring to near relatives (see MM) It is possible, therefore, that "his Own" (ὁ ἴδιος) was a title that early Christians gave to Jesus, comparable to "the Beloved" (ὁ ἀγαπητός); compare Ro 8.32, where Paul refers to God "who did not spare τοῦ ἰδίου υἱοῦ" in a context that clearly alludes to Gn 22.16, where the Septuagint has τοῦ ἀγαπητοῦ υἱοῦ.[5]

Metzger's comments indicate that a number of scholars believe the expression "through the blood of his own" (διὰ τοῦ αἵματος τοῦ ἰδίου) is an echo of a larger story understood by all in Israel in the second temple period. This is, of course, the story of the *akeda* or "binding" of Isaac. We have already seen in our study of the voice at the baptism of Jesus (chapter 2) a likely echo of the story told in Genesis 22 in the use of the phrase "the beloved" (ὁ ἀγαπητός). And we have noted the reference to the story of the sacrifice of Isaac by several New Testament writers. But debate continues about whether a developed Jewish theology of the vicarious and redemptive significance of Isaac's sacrifice existed in the second temple period. Some have suggested that our available Jewish sources from the period do indicate such a developed theology. In particular, Geza Vermes has long argued in favor of this view.[6] Others have cast doubts on this assertion. For example, Joseph Fitzmyer, comment-

---

3. Hort, and Westcott, *The New Testament in the Original Greek: Notes on Selected Readings*, 98–100.

4. Bruce, *Acts*, 361.

5. Metzger, *Textual Commentary*, 426.

6. Vermes, *Scripture and Tradition*, 109–13.

ing on Rom 8:32, reviews the controversy and concludes that "the tradition of the death and ashes of Isaac and his subsequent resurrection can be reasonably understood as an attempt to enrich Judaism with a figure that was as colorful as the one known to Christian exegesis."[7] It is no surprise to find Fitzmyer, in his comment on the textual problem at Acts 20:28, referring to this special sense of "his own dear one" (τοῦ ἰδίου) as "a last ditch solution to this text-critical problem."[8] Did the later Jewish exegetes simply transfer to Isaac what the Christians had claimed about Jesus, or were the earliest Christians drawing on an already developed and powerful story that was current in first century Judaism? Our extant sources point to the latter.

One important piece of evidence for the antiquity of this tradition comes from *Jub* 17:15. In this re-telling of the Genesis story, written in the second century BCE, we read that God's order to Abraham took place on the twelfth day of the first month, i.e., 12th Nisan. The site of the sacrifice was reached on the third day (i.e., 15th Nisan: *Jub.* 18:3). Thus for *Jubilees* the sacrifice of Isaac took place at the time of Passover. The redemptive significance of the sacrifice, given this added information, would hardly have been lost on any Jew of the period. Already by the time of Jesus the sacrifice of Isaac was linked to the Passover. We also note that the *Book of Jubilees* identifies the "one of the mountains that I shall show you" of Gen 22:2 as Mount Moriah, which is the name given for the temple mount in 2 Chr 3:1.

According to Vermes, further evidence for a developed theology of the "binding" of Isaac can be found in the fragment from the Dead Sea Scrolls, 4Q225.[9] This fragment offers a re-telling of the story of Gen 22 that is similar to the one found in *Jubilees*. The Qumran fragment adds several details to the biblical account: the presence of Angels, including the angels of Mastema, who stand over against God, the crying angels, and the fire and bright cloud. Vermes also suggests that the document may offer pre-Christian currency to the traditions that Isaac consents and asks to be bound, and hints at the merits of Isaac's sacrifice. Whether these latter elements are included as part of the developed Isaac theology in 4Q225 is debatable, due to the fragmentary nature of the docu-

---

7. Fitzmyer, *Romans*, 532, citing A. F. Segal, "He who Did Not Spare," 169–84.

8. Fitzmyer, *Acts*, 680.

9. Vermes, *Jewish Context*, 109–13. See especially the table on 113, which sets out evidence for a developed theology of the story before the rise of Christianity.

ment, but there can be little doubt that the Qumran fragment follows fairly closely the story as found in *Jubilees,* and thus it has been called *Pseudo-Jubilees.*

Elements of the developed story of the sacrifice of Isaac have also been found in the writings of Josephus (*Ant* 1, 222–36) and in the *Liber Antiquitatem Biblicarum (LAB)* also known as Pseudo-Philo, 18:5; 32:2–4; 40:2. Elements of the developed Isaac tradition can also be found in the Palestinian Targum.[10] It has influenced the mid-first century Jewish persecution tractate 4 Macc 13:12; 16:20:

> Remember whence you came, and the father by whose hand Isaac would have submitted to being slain for the sake of religion [for the sake of God] . . . For his sake also our father Abraham was zealous to sacrifice His son Isaac, the ancestor of our nation; and when Isaac saw his father's hand wielding the knife, and descending upon him, he did not cower.

Here the martyrs are likened to Isaac, who willingly submitted "for the sake of religion." Elsewhere in the tractate the faithfulness of the martyrs is considered to be a "ransom" (ἀντίψυχον). In 6:29 the martyred priest Eleazar prays "make my blood their purification" (ἀντίψυχον), and take my life in exchange for theirs." In 17:21–22 the martyrs' death is related to the redemption of the nation:

> The tyrant was punished, and the homeland purified–they having become, as it were a ransom (ἀντίψυχον) for the sin of the nation , and through the blood of those devout ones and their death as an atoning sacrifice (ἱλαστήριου) divine Providence preserved Israel that previously had been mistreated.

Although some scholars have criticized Vermes' confidence regarding the extent of this developed *Akedah* tradition in second temple Judaism,[11] there can be little doubt that a redemptive theology focused on the near-sacrifice of Isaac and nurtured in the matrix of martyrdom and persecution formed a part of the mental furniture of Jewish thought of the time before CE 70. This heightened interest and developed interpretation of

---

10. Ibid., 113.

11. Davies and Chilton, "The Akedah," 514–46. For fuller bibliography see Vermes, *Jewish Context,* 183 n. 23. Campbell, *Story114,* for recent discussion and critique of Davies and Chilton.

Genesis 22 is found in first century Judaism in "a broad array of sources of various genres and different locales."[12]

But there is more evidence to consider from Paul's speech in Acts 20 that has relevance for the text-critical question. In particular, Paul echoes Ps 74:2 in verse 28: "to shepherd the church of God that he obtained with the blood of his own Son." Psalm 74:2 (73:2 LXX)[13] prays to God, "Remember your congregation, which you acquired long ago; you redeemed the staff of your heritage." A closer look at the Ps 74 as a whole, and the story of Israel that it narrates, yields some interesting results. Psalm 74 is a community lament over the destruction of Jerusalem, probably the destruction by the Babylonians in 587 BCE, and the silencing of prophecy, "one of the most disorienting blows of all."[14] Mays suggests that it was likely composed during the Babylonian exile that followed "for performances at services of mourning over the destroyed temple in Jerusalem."[15] In between the lament over this destruction (vv. 1–11) and the plea for God to act in vindication of his name and covenant (vv. 18–23) the gloom and despair is relieved by a recitation of God's ancient exploits in creation and in redeeming his people (vv. 12–17). This fresh theological perspective in the midst of the most devastating circumstances is anticipated in verse 2,

> Remember your congregation,
> Which you acquired long ago,
> Which you redeemed to be the tribe of your heritage,
> Remember Mount Zion, where you came to dwell.

The reference here is obviously to the deliverance from bondage in Egypt, which included the Passover, the crossing of the Red Sea, the journey through the wilderness, and the crossing of the Jordan into the promised land. This becomes clear in verses 12–17.

> [12] Yet God is my King of old,
> Working salvation in the earth.
> [13] You divided the sea by your might;
> You broke the heads of the dragons in the waters,
> [14] You crushed the heads of Leviathan;
> You gave him as food for the creatures of the wilderness.

---

12. Levenson, *Death and Resurrection*, 176.
13. *NETS*, 583.
14. Kidner, *Psalms*, 265.
15. Mays, *Psalms*, 244.

¹⁵ You cut openings for springs and torrents;
You dried up ever-flowing streams.
¹⁶ Yours is the day, yours also the night,
You established the luminaries and the sun.
¹⁷ You fixed all the bounds of the earth;
You made summer and winter.

This theological outburst in the midst of unmitigated gloom serves to remind Israel of who God is and what he has done in the face of present and primordial chaos. The God who delivered Israel out of Egypt is the same God who brought order out of the ancient chaos. He is the one who can yet deliver no matter what wild beasts (dragons, Leviathan) may ravage. This is the *story* that is told by Psalm 74, and it is the same *story* that Paul is narrating in his speech to the Ephesian elders: The God who delivered Israel out of Egypt, and smote the great beasts, is the God who has delivered them "by the blood of his own dear one," and will yet deliver them when "savage wolves will come in among you not sparing the flock" (Acts 20:29). So then, if we foreground Psalm 74, noting that not only the language but the logic of the psalm has influenced the speech in Acts 20, we will gain both a deeper appreciation of the theology of the speech and some further clues in deciding on this textual crux.

First, as we have already seen, the reference to *the blood of his own* (τοῦ αἵματος τοῦ ἰδίου) has been seen by some scholars as a technical term, and by others as an echo of the story of Genesis 22. The fact that this peculiar expression is linked with a reference to the deliverance of Israel from Egypt in the speech using words reminiscent of Ps 74:2 should not escape our notice. It is to be noted that the words used in Acts 20:28 are not the same as those of LXX Ps 73:2, but the idea of God's obtaining his people with blood can hardly be other than the reference to the Passover. If this is so, then at Acts 20:28 we may hear Paul (as represented by Luke) linking the sacrifice of Isaac and the Passover. So the wording in UBS⁴/NA²⁷ *the church of God which he purchased with the blood of his own dear one* makes good narrative sense of the passage, and confirms that this is likely the original wording here. Deeper appreciation of the story has helped to establish the text.

Then there is the reference to *savage wolves* (λύκοι βαρεῖς). In an essay entitled "Grievous Wolves (Acts 20:29)" G. W. H. Lampe explored the use of this terminology in early Christianity.¹⁶ He argues that the

---

16. Lampe, "Grievous Wolves," 253–68.

terminology is habitually applied to false prophets in the first and second centuries, and that this is the likely connotation in Paul's speech to the Ephesian elders. In light of this plausible interpretation, it is worth noting that in Psalm 74 among the complaints the Psalmist makes is that "there is no longer any prophet" (Ps 74:9). The closest Old Testament parallel to this passage is Lam 2, in which the mourning over the destruction of Jerusalem is followed by the complaint in 2:14:

> Your prophets have seen for you
> False and deceptive visions:
> They have not exposed your iniquity
> To restore your fortunes
> But have seen oracles for you
> That are false and misleading.

The cry of Ps 74:9 may refer not so much to the loss of all prophecy, but to the fact that the only prophets left are false prophets. This is precisely what Paul is warning against in Acts 20:29.

One other factor is worth considering regarding the text of Acts 20:28 and the echo of Psalm 74. If the volume of the echo for writer and audience is very high, it is worth noting that habitually it is "God" (θεὸς) who is addressed in the Psalm. By contrast, "the Lord" (κύριος) is used only once for certain (LXX Ps 73:18).[17] Here may be further support for τοῦ θεοῦ as the original reading at Acts 20:28.

But another Old Testament passage may also be echoed in Acts 20:28. A number of commentators have discerned that the word "obtained" (περιεποιήσατο) is an echo of Isa 43:21:

> The people whom I have formed for myself
> So that they might declare my praise.[18]

This identification of an echo of Isaiah 43 in Paul's speech to the Ephesian elders is made more plausible due to the importance of this passage from Isaiah in early Christian preaching and apologetic.[19] And if an echo of Isaiah 43 can be heard in Acts 20, then it appears that Paul (in Luke's representation) constructs his speech as an exposition of three scrip-

---

17. LXX Ps 73:8 reads κύριος but Ms. S gives the variant θεὸς.
18. Lake and Cadbury, *Beginnings* (IV), 261; Bruce, *Acts*, 393 n. 65. Earlier commentators include Lightfoot, *Notes*, 76.
19. Dodd, *According to the Scriptures*, 90 notes 6 echoes of Isaiah 43 in the New Testament, but does not include Acts 20:28.

ture passages: Genesis 22 (Torah); Isaiah 43 (Prophets); and Psalm 74 (Writings).

In light of these considerations, the other textual variation in Acts 20:28 deserves re-consideration. Some "Western" witnesses read "for himself" (ἑαυτῷ).[20] Although Fitzmyer deems the reading to be "an insignificant addition,"[21] we may discern behind it the expression "for myself" (Heb לִי). What on first reading appears to be an insignificant scribal gloss may turn out, on closer inspection, to be a significant echo of Isa 43:21.

## TRANSMISSION HISTORY

Acts 20:28 is rich in Old Testament echoes, and these may well provide clues to the narrative and theological substructure of the whole speech. They may also provide clues to the transmission history and the textual crux of the verse. The link between the near-sacrifice of Isaac and the deliverance from Egypt, together with God's obtaining for himself a people in delivering them from exile (Isaiah 43) drew on key elements of Israel's story and would have had a powerful impact on the elders at Ephesus and the early readers of Acts. But as the text was copied in new contexts, especially in an increasingly gentile church, the echoes would have become more faint and the story less available to readers and hearers. "His own dear one" would not have as easily been recognized as a reference to Isaac as a type of Christ. The strong link in Judaism between Genesis 22 and the Passover/Exodus would not have been heard with the same force of a redemptive theology with which the link had been associated in Judaism (*Jubilees*, 4Q225, 4 Maccabees). The nexus of these important scriptural allusions, and the passages they evoke, would be less noticed. The echoes would become more faint.

As the underlying story was lost, the text began to change. New challenges placed new pressures on the text and its copyists. The Patripassianist teaching that God himself suffered, and shed blood, in Christ's death would tempt scribes to alter "God" (θεοῦ) to "Lord" (κυρίου) or to change the wording of "through the blood his own dear one" (διὰ τοῦ αἵματος τοῦ ἰδίου). The tendency in the earliest manuscripts to omit unnecessary words would have endangered "for himself"

---

20. P⁴¹ ᵛⁱᵈ D Ir^Lat.
21. Fitzmyer, *Acts*, 680.

(ἑαυτῷ) once it was no longer heard as an echo of Isa 43:21. In these new copying situations in the early church there was an "eclipse of the biblical narrative," to adopt Hans Frei's phrase. But the recovery of Israel's story, key elements of which are indicated in the scriptural echoes in Paul's speech to the Ephesian elders, offers valuable clues to the textual-critic exegete and theologian.

# 7

## Philippians 4:7

OUR PRINTED EDITIONS AND translations of the New Testament read that the peace of God that passes understanding will "keep your hearts and minds in Christ Jesus." A few manuscripts add "and your bodies" (καὶ τὰ σώματα ὑμῶν ). E. Lohmeyer had suggested that the reading καὶ τὰ σώματα was what Paul wrote at Phil 4:7, arguing that it fit the theme of martyrdom, which he believed undergirded the letter. Others have not followed him, and Lohmeyer himself admitted that the manuscript evidence for the reading was insufficient.[1] However, M. Silva has recently noted, "The variant should not be dismissed too quickly . . . Accounting for the change from "minds" (νοήματα) to "bodies" (σώματα) is rather difficult."[2]

### MANUSCRIPT EVIDENCE

The addition of papyrus P[16] to the list of authorities supporting the reading "and your bodies" (καὶ τὰ σώματα ὑμῶν) considerably strengthens the case for considering it original. P[16] is listed by the editors of UBS[4]/NA[27] as apparently supporting the reading in conflation. The original editors noted "the ordinary reading here is καὶ τὰ νοήματα, but F and G and some other minor authorities substitute σώματα for νοήματα. The papyrus is peculiar in having both."[3] Peculiar, perhaps, but not singular. The conflation is also found in some manuscripts of the vulgate.

P[16] (P. Oxy 1009) is a late third or early fourth century papyrus containing Philippians 3 and 4. According to one recent estimate this

---

1. Lohmeyer, *Philipper*, 167, 170–72.
2. Silva, *Philippians*, 199.
3. Grenfel and Hunt, *Oxyrhynchus Papyri 7*, 11.

papyrus demonstrates approximately 80 percent agreement with ℵ and B.[4] The Alands listed P[16] in their category I, "manuscripts of a very special quality which should always be considered in establishing the original text."[5] P[16] probably originated in Egypt and represents the normal Alexandrian text. Since the conflated reading is also supported by several manuscripts of the vulgate, we may conclude that it was preserved in both the east and the west and has early attestation.

## TRANSCRIPTIONAL PROBABILITIES

In presenting the textual data for Phil 4:7, UBS[4] suggests that the omission of "and your minds" (καὶ τὰ νοήματα ὑμῶν) in 263 *1590 1809* it[b] vg[ms] Origen[lat1/3]; Ambrosiaster Hillary was due to *homoioteleuton*, or similar line ending. This is a reasonable suggestion, but it is equally as plausible for the omission of "and your bodies" (καὶ τὰ σώματα ὑμῶν) from the large majority of witnesses. That such omissions were common in the great uncials, especially ℵ (Sinaiticus) was demonstrated long ago by A. C. Clark.[6] Moreover, we note that elsewhere in Philippians P[46] is capable of such an omission due to similar line ending. In Phil 3:14 the scribe has omitted "in Christ Jesus" (ἐν Χριστῷ Ἰησοῦ). Gordon Fee suggests that *homoioteleuton* is the cause.[7] If the exemplar(s) of P[46] ℵ and B was as prone to this phenomenon as its descendants (What manuscript was wholly free of it?), then we may conclude that both "and your minds" (καὶ τὰ νοήματα ὑμῶν) and "and your bodies" (καὶ τὰ σώματα ὑμῶν) were omitted from Phil 4:7 in the course of transmission, and that the conflated text, as found in P[16] has a claim to be original.

It has been suggested that the cause of textual alteration in Phil 4:7 may have been intentional rather than accidental. Peter O'Brien suggested that "Later scribes may have changed νοήματα to σώματα if they thought that νοήματα after καρδίας was redundant."[8]

Yet another motive might have been at work in the transmission of the text: namely asceticism. Kim Haines-Eitzen has noted that the theme of the body was a central idea in early Christian discussion, and

---

4. Comfort and Barrett, *The Text*, 93.
5. Aland and Aland, *Text of the New Testament*, 105.
6. Clark, *Primitive Text*, 24–32.
7. Fee, *Philippians*, 338 n. 6.
8. O'Brien, *Philippians*, 483.

has argued that the body is the organizing idea behind the collection in *Bodmer Papyrus VII–IX*, known to New Testament students as P[72]. Haines-Eitzen wrote concerning this theme:

> The theme became so crucial for the early church with the bewildering variety of ascetic choices. Contests over "bodies" and "texts" were, in fact, remarkably interwoven in the arena of early Christian theological debates. Does Christ have a real body? Does God have a body? Is there a resurrection of the flesh? Such were the questions that drove intense combat among patristic writers and desert monks.[9]

So we might be drawn to the suggestion that in the context of a high-stakes debate over the body a scribe would be tempted to add "and your bodies."(καὶ τὰ σώματα ὑμῶν) at Phil 4:7. But attractive (and fashionable) as such a theory might be, it seems unlikely. In all probability the reading was current in the tradition prior to the rise of controversies over the "body" or the monastic movement. It dates at least to the third, and probably to the second century.

## INTERNAL CRITERIA

A further consideration has to do with a stylistic feature of the letter. Elsewhere in Philippians Paul lists three items together. For example, in 2:25 he refers to Epaphroditus as his "brother, and co-worker, and fellow-soldier." Similarly, three items appear in 2:10, "in heaven, and on earth, and under the earth," although here Paul may be quoting from a hymn. Phil 4:18 might also be an example. Here Paul writes, "I have been paid in full and have more than enough. I am fully satisfied." To find three items together at Phil 4:7 would be in line with Paul's usage elsewhere in the epistle (see also Phil 3:2).

## NARRATIVE FEATURES

But another line of inquiry may be fruitful. UBS[4] gives a marginal reference at Phil 4:7 to Isa 26:3: "Those of steadfast mind you keep in peace . . . in peace because they trust in you."

Isaiah 26 was an important scripture passage for inter-testamental Judaism. The crucial verse was 26:19: "Your dead shall live, their corpses shall rise."

---

9. Haines-Eitzen, *Guardians of Letters*, 103.

Concerning this verse and the context in which it is found N. T. Wright has recently observed, "The original Hebrew refers literally to the bodily Resurrection, and this is certainly how the verse is taken in the LXX and at Qumran."[10]

In Isaiah 25–26 several ideas merge: restoration of Israel, eschatological hope, and individual bodily resurrection. That these themes were of concern to Paul can hardly be doubted. But especially prominent in Philippians was the idea of bodily resurrection. We note especially the statement at the close of chapter 3:

> He will transform the body of our humiliation that it may be conformed to the body of his glory by the power that also enables him to make all things subject to himself.
>
> (ὃς μετασχηματίσει τὸ σῶμα τῆς ταπεινώσεως ἡμῶν σύμμορφον τῷ σώματι τῆς δόξης αὐτοῦ κατὰ τὴν ἐνέργειαν τοῦ δύνασθαι αὐτὸν καὶ ὑποτάξαι αὐτῷ τὰ πάντα).

Earlier in the chapter Paul had spoken of knowing the power of Christ's resurrection (3:10) and desired to attain the resurrection of the dead (3:11). But the only other place where the word body σῶμα is used in Philippians is in 1:20, where Paul speaks of Christ being glorified in his body (μεγαλυνθήσεται Χριστὸς ἐν τῷ σώματί μου). This emphasis on the resurrection of the body in Philippians suggests that the reference to bodies here is in line with Paul's thought.

I would contend, then, that Paul included three items in Phil 4:7, as a conscious echo of Isa 26:3. With this echo Paul had in mind the larger concern of the context, so familiar to the Jews of the period, and that bodily resurrection is clearly in view. The original text is found in the conflated reading, preserved in P[16], and a few vulgate manuscripts. The original read "your hearts and your minds and your bodies" (τὰς καρδίας ὑμῶν καὶ τὰ νοήματα ὑμῶν καὶ τὰ σώματα ὑμῶν). Each of the last two elements was omitted at some stage of the transmission by *homoioteleuton*. To read the full text is to hear not later church squabbles about the body, but the Apostle Paul speak of the peace that comes from the God who raised Jesus from the dead, and who will change our lowly bodies to be fashioned like his own glorious body.

One early Christian writer who preserved the reading "and your bodies" (καὶ τὰ σώματα ὑμῶν) and reflected on Paul's view of the resur-

---

10. Wright, *Resurrection*, 117.

rection body in this context was Victorinus. Tischendorf cites this late fourth century writer in his eighth edition of the Greek New Testament:[11]

> *Ecce et hic significatio est de resurrectione corpora, inquit, vestra in Iesu Christo: in ipsius enim maiestate et virtute corpora nostra sunt, quae cum eius adventu resurgent, reviviscent, merita accipient* . . . etc.
>
> And behold this is a sign of the resurrection of your bodies, it is said, in Jesus Christ: indeed in himself are the majesty and power of our bodies, who with his coming will rise and revive and receive merit . . . etc.

It appears that Victorinus had understood the theological heart of the Apostle Paul, the gospel of the Resurrection according to the scriptures.

## TRANSMISSION HISTORY

The proposal I have made regarding the longer text of Phil 4:7 suggests the following transmission history. Paul originally wrote three items, affirming that the peace of God would keep "their hearts and their minds and their bodies." Some time before the end of the second century a careless scribe failed to copy the last words "and your bodies," a mistake caused by similar line ending. The resulting text made perfect sense, and the echo of Isaiah 26 was not of sufficient volume to copyists less attuned to intertextual echo than Paul and his readers. If we hear again the echo, we may be alert to the full theological weight of Paul's statement. The bodily resurrection of Jesus was the guarantee of the scriptural promise, "Your dead shall live, their bodies shall rise" (Isa 26:19).

11 Tischendorf, *Novum Testamentum*, 2:723.

# 8

# Romans 8:2

COMMENTATORS HAVE BEEN DIVIDED on the text of Rom 8:2. Did Paul write "you" singular (σε) "me" (με) or "us" (ἡμᾶς) when referring to the liberation in Christ Jesus from the law of sin and death? Was it "you" (singular),"me," or "we" who gained the deliverance? The third option, "us" (ἡμᾶς) lacks sufficient external support to have commended it to modern critics. The choice in between σε and με. Both have substantial support in the manuscript tradition.

For σε: ℵ B G 1739*
For με: ADKP

One recently published uncial (0311) adds support to the reading με.[1]

## MANUSCRIPT EVIDENCE

In the last half century the scales have been tipped in favor of σε. It is interesting to note the judgment and degree of certainty for this reading given by the United Bible Societies committee in their four successive editions of the Greek New Testament:

UBS (1966) με {C}
UBS² (1968) με {C}
UBS³ (1975) σε {D}
UBS⁴ (1994) σε {B}

The pronoun σε seems generally to hold the field among critics. Given the lack of papyri for this verse, the weight of ℵ B will have been considered by some to be superior.[2] But others will agree with Fitzmyer that

---

1. Head, "Five New Testament Manuscripts," 521–45.
2. Fee, *Presence*, 519 n. 134.

"the extrinsic testimony in support of these readings is almost equal."[3] The new evidence of manuscript 0311 makes the balance of extrinsic support more even still. The decision is usually taken by modern editors on the basis of intrinsic and transcriptional probabilities.

## TRANSCRIPTIONAL PROBABILITIES

Several transcriptional scenarios have been suggested regarding this variation. In favor of σε it is noted that a scribe would be tempted to conform Rom 8:2 to reflect the με of the preceding passage. Brendan Byrne concluded: "The variant *set me free* (A D) is to be rejected as an assimilation to the sustained use of the first person in 7:7–25."[4] On the other hand, B. M. Metzger noted the argument frequently cited by those who prefer με: "σε may have originated in the accidental repetition of the final syllable of ἠλευθέρωσέν when the the terminal—ν, represented by a horizontal line over the ε was overlooked.[5] Metzger also noted the position, proposed by F. J. A. Hort and adopted by C. K. Barrett, that there was originally no pronoun, and those in the manuscript tradition were added as attempts at stylistic improvement. But there is no manuscript evidence for this suggestion. Barrett adds, "Fortunately the variation makes no difference whatever to the meaning of the sentence."[6] I hope this essay will show that there is a significant difference, depending on our choice of reading.

## INTERNAL CRITERIA

The textual question is unlikely to be solved by appeals either to external support or to transcriptional probabilities. Internal criteria must be considered, namely the theology, style and rhetoric of the letter. Stanley Stowers has offered a reading of Romans that in his view "resolves a longstanding textual dilemma" at 8:2. Stowers argues that in Romans 7, as elsewhere in the letter, Paul is employing a standard rhetorical convention of the Greco-Roman world called *prosopopoiia* (speech in character). This is a literary or rhetorical technique in which the writer produces speech that represents not himself or herself but another per-

---

3. Fitzmyer, *Romans*, 483.
4. Byrne, *Romans*, 242.
5. Metzger, *Textual Commentary*, 456.
6. Barrett, *Romans*, 144.

son or type of character.[7] *Prosopopoiia* was a well-established rhetorical convention in the early empire for which evidence is found in Cicero, Quintillian, the *Progymnastica* of Theon, and Aphthonius. Origin understood Paul to be following this rhetorical convention in Romans 7, but the later interpreters who were unaware of *prosopopoiia* failed to see that Paul was addressing another person in this way. Especially in the West, beginning with Augustine, the passage was interpreted as Paul's introspection. Stowers, then, sees the "you" (singular) of Rom 8:2 as a continuation of the *prosopopoiia* rhetorical style of chapter 7, and for him the textual problem is solved. For Stowers, the singular "you" is the person Paul is addressing.[8]

Stowers' proposal on the text of Rom 8:2, however attractive, is not without problems. First of all, one must ask, if the "me" (με) form served for "speech in character" in Rom 7:7–25, why should Paul abandon it at Rom 8:2? Secondly, both Origen and Didymus recognized that Paul was employing *prosopopoiia* in Romans 7.[9] But both read με in 8:2. Furthermore, Stowers asserts that Paul, like other ancient writers, is echoing in 7:24–25, a passage from Euripides *Medea* (1077–80). This is the classic text for the discussion of *akrasia*, the weakness of the will, in Greek and Roman sources. The passage describes a woman tempted to a revenge plot that includes the death of her children: "I am being overcome by evils. I know that what I am about to do is evil, but passion is stronger than my reasoned reflection and this is the cause of the worst evils for humans."[10]

While it may be admitted that Paul is *formally* indebted to the convention of *prosopopoiia* and is doubtless aware of the discussion of *akrasia* in Greek and Roman literature, he certainly shows no substantive dependence on this text of Euripides. For the *narrative* subtext of Paul's discussion in Rom 7:7—8:4 we must look elsewhere.

## NARRATIVE FEATURES

I offer, then, an alternative proposal which seems to me to be much more satisfactory, and produces some surprising results. I believe that Paul is

7. Stowers, *Rereading*, 16–17.
8. Ibid., 282.
9. Ibid., 268.
10. Ibid., 260.

indebted here, and elsewhere, to the logic and pattern of the Psalms of lament, including what are called "the Psalms of the righteous sufferer" and the "penitential Psalms."

My own thinking on the shape of the psalms and their influence on the New Testament text was sparked by an observation of Brevard Childs on Psalm 30, "The psalmist originally described his own desperate plight and how God brought up his soul from Sheol in deliverance. He then called on the faithful to give praise to God."[11]

A number of psalms take this shape including Psalm 22 and Psalm 69 (both very important to New Testament writers). The psalm begins with the cry of an individual, alone and in distress, either because of sin or because of enemies, and ends with that person redeemed and leading the company of God's people in praise. A quintessential short example of this pattern is found in Psalm 130. Then I noticed that in its shape Romans 7–8 conforms to this pattern. The "wretched man" of 7:24 becomes the one who writes in 8:39 that nothing "will be able to separate *us* from the love of God in Christ Jesus our Lord." Then, looking more closely at the narrative shape of Psalm 130 I saw a striking correspondence with the narrative shape of Romans 7–11. Consider the following: (NRSV)

> Ps 130:1–3: Out of the depths I cry to you, O Lord. Lord, hear my voice! Let your ears be attentive to the voice of my supplications! If you, O Lord, should mark iniquities, Lord, who could stand?

> Rom 7:21, 24: So I find it to be a law that when I want to do good, evil lies close at hand... Wretched man that I am! Who will rescue me from this body of death?

> Ps 130:4: But there is forgiveness with you, so that you may be revered.

> Rom 7:25, 8:1: Thanks be to God trough Jesus Christ our Lord.... There is therefore now no condemnation for those who are in Christ Jesus. For the law of the Spirit of life in Christ Jesus has set me free....

> Ps 130:5–6: I wait for the Lord, my soul waits, and in his word I hope; My soul waits for the Lord more than those who watch for the morning, more than those who watch for the morning.

---

11. Childs, *Introduction*, 519.

> Rom 8:23-25 ... We ourselves, who have the first fruits of the Spirit, groan inwardly while we wait for adoption, the redemption of our bodies. For in hope we were saved. Now hope that is seen is not hope. For who hopes for what is seen? But if we hope for what we do not see, we wait for it with patience.
>
> Ps 130:7-8: O Israel, hope in the Lord! For with the Lord there is steadfast love, And with him is great power to redeem. It is he who will redeem Israel from all its iniquities.
>
> Rom 9-11 (especially 11:26-27): And so all Israel shall be saved, as it is written. Out Of Zion will come the Deliverer; and will banish ungodliness from Jacob. And this is my covenant with them, when I take away their sins.

It seems that the narrative shape of Ps 130 has, either consciously or subconsciously, influenced the movement of Paul's thought throughout the whole of Romans 7-11.

There is, however, one outlier to this satisfying fit between Psalm 130 and Romans 7-11. The problem comes in verse 4, where the psalmist writes, "But there is forgiveness with you, so that you may be revered." The idea of *fear* seems to be at odds with Paul's thought in Rom 8:15: "For you did not receive a spirit of slavery to fall back into fear, but you have received the spirit of adoption..."

It is here, however, at Ps 130:4 that there is a notable textual variation that has a bearing on my proposal. Whereas the MT reads "so that you may be reveared," i.e., feared, the Greek Old Testament gives a variety of translations. LXX ℵ A reads "on account of your name" (ἕνεκεν τοῦ ὀνόματός σου). Codex B is defective here, as is the great Psalms scroll from Qumran. LXX ms R (The Verona Greek-Latin Psalter of the sixth century) reads "law" (νόμου), as do Symmachus and Theodotian, while Aquila, following the Masoretic text, reads "fear" (φόβον). As for the other columns of the hexapla, Jerome noted that quinta read *terroem*, sexta read *verbum*.[12] Jerome suggested that the difficulty arose through a confusion of the Hebrew letters *waw* and *yod* (Epistles, 106), and his translations reflect the variety: Juxta Hebr: *cum teribilis sis*; Juxta LXX: *propter legem tuam*. This is also the reading of the *Roman Psalter*.[13] Variations are also found in the Targum, reading, "that you may ap-

---

12. Jellico, *The Septuagint*, 121.
13. Weber, *Le Psautier Romain*, 321.

pear, be seen."[14] Albert Pietersma's translation, "for the sake of your law," reflects the reading in Rhalfs' manual edition, (in contrast to his critical edition of the Psalms in the Gottingen edition) a translation which aims to represent "the Greek text as it left the hands of its respective translators."[15] It is reasonable to suppose, then, that the reading "on account of your law." (ἕνεκεν τοῦ νόμου σου) was current in Paul's time, was known to him, and fits well with the discussion of the Law in Romans 7.

On the level of vocabulary, we note several interesting correspondences between Psalm 130 (129 LXX) and Romans 7–11. First of all, the specific malady in Psalm 129 LXX is "lawlessness" (ἀνομία) both of the individual (vs 3) and of Israel (vs 8). We note Paul's phrase in 6:19, "greater and greater iniquity" (τῇ ἀνομίᾳ εἰς τὴν ἀνομίαν), and his use of the term in 4:7, citing Ps 32:1-2. Then there is the word for mercy (ἔλεος) and its cognates, a key term for Psalm 129 LXX and for Romans 9–11. The climax of Paul's story is "that God may have mercy of all" (ἵνα τοὺς πάντας ἐλεήσῃ), Rom 11:32.

In addition, we notice that the word "depth" (βάθος) is found in Ps 129:1 (LXX) to describe the intensity of the psalmist's lament. It is interesting to note that this word occurs only 4 times in the undoubted Pauline letters. The two in Romans are at 8:39, "neither height nor depth...", and 11:33, " O depth of wealth..." I suggest that the βάθος of Rom 8:39 and 11:33 is an answer to the βάθος (though the word itself is not used) in Rom 7:24.

I propose, then, that Psalm 130 offers the narrative substructure to Rom 7:7—11:36, and that this assists in establishing "me" (με) as the original reading of Rom 8:2. The close verbal and conceptual links suggest that Psalm 130 functions like "a massive reef, hidden just below the waterline," to borrow the felicitous analogy of Ross Wagner.[16]

But this way of looking at this long section of Paul's letter to the Romans has a bearing on the much-discussed problem of the "I" in Rom 7:7-24. Fitzmyer gives a thorough outline of five possible interpretations,[17] and suggests, as others had before him a background for Paul's discussion in Romans 7 in the hymns at Qumran. But it is more likely that both Paul and Qumran are drawing on the biblical Psalms of lament,

14. Stec, *Targum of the Psalms*, 226.
15. *NETS*, xix, 612.
16. Wagner, *Herald*, 203.
17. Fitzmyer, *Romans*, 463–66.

including the penitential Psalm 130. The general trend in interpretation is away from thinking of Paul as referring to himself, and more of Paul using a rhetorical convention, or of speaking of humanity in general or of the experience of Israel. The so-called "psychological-autobiographical" interpretation of Romans 7 has not fared well in the last century. It received a heavy blow from Werner George Kümmel in 1929,[18] and what many consider the final stroke with Krister Stendahl's 1962 essay, "The Apostle Paul and the Introspective Conscience of the West." Stendahl argues that the Western interpretation, beginning with Augustine and championed by Luther, seriously misunderstood Paul, who elsewhere gives evidence of a "robust conscience" (Philippians 3) rather than an introspective one.[19] But if the narrative substructure of Romans 7 and the chapters that follow may be found in Psalm 130, which Luther called one of the "Pauline psalms" (together with Psalm 32, Psalm 51, and Psalm 143, all quoted in Romans), then Stendahl's view needs to be reassessed. The personal awareness of being a sinner before God, and of God's remedy of the problem, as found in Psalm 130, opens out to a word of hope and expectation for the redemption of Israel. The Psalm's "story" fits well with the broader narrative shape of Romans 7–11 and indicates that "me" (με) is what Paul wrote in Rom 8:2.[20]

## TRANSMISSION HISTORY

This study suggests the following transmission history at Rom 8:2. Paul originally wrote "set me free," but accidental confusion led an early scribe to alter the text to "you" singular. Subsequent copyists and commentators, not attuned to an echo of Psalm 130, were less inclined to hear Paul speak of his deep anguish and his remarkable freedom, both for himself and for Israel. Modern interpreters, uncomfortable with Paul's "introspection," have failed to hear the story that shaped the text.

---

18. Kümmel, *Romer*.
19. Stendahl, *Paul*, 78–96.
20. An earlier version of this chapter was given as a paper for the Paul and Pauline Letters seminar at the SBL International conference in Rome on July 3, 2009.

# 9

## Mark 9:29

This study will argue that the reading "prayer and fasting" is what Mark originally wrote, and that larger narrative features in the story of the healing of the boy with the spirit supports this reading.

### MANUSCRIPT EVIDENCE

Most manuscripts of Mark read, "This kind can only be cast out by prayer and fasting." A few important manuscripts lack the words "and fasting." These are:

> ℵ* The original hand of Codex Sinaiticus (fourth century)
> B Codex Vaticanus (fourth century)
> 0274 (fifth century)
> 2427 (fourteenth century?)
> it$^k$ African Latin Codex Bobbiensis (c. 400)
> geo$^1$ First revision of the Georgian version.
> Clement of Alexandria

The support of Sinaiticus and Vaticanus, together with the early African Latin manuscript, Codex Bobbiensis, is sufficiently weighty for most modern scholars to adopt the shorter reading against the vast majority of manuscripts. Many modern commentators dismiss the longer reading with a footnote. For example, A. Y. Collins, in her recent commentary on Mark, writes of "the shorter reading attested by ℵ* B et al," thus masking how very slender is the external manuscript support for the shorter reading.[1] However, not all contemporary scholars dismiss the textual question so easily. R. T. France notes the "massive external evidence" for the longer reading and suggests, "They should perhaps be retained,

---

1. Collins, *Mark*, 434.

despite the confident A-rating of UBS⁴ (unless it is believed that ℵ and B together can never be wrong!)"[2]

## TRANSCRIPTIONAL PROBABILITIES

Bruce Metzger recorded the consensus of the UBS committee with regard to the transcriptional probabilities at Mark 9:29. "In light of the increasing emphasis in the early church on the necessity of fasting, it is understandable that καὶ νηστείᾳ is a gloss that found its way into most witnesses."[3] Metzger adds fuller comment in his book *The Text of the New Testament*: "It is not surprising that monks in their work of transcribing manuscripts, should have introduced several references to fasting. This has happened in numerous manuscripts at Mark 9.29, Acts 10.30 and 1 Cor. 7.5."[4] However, the almost universal attestation of "prayer and fasting" in the manuscript tradition of Mark 9:29 makes it clear that the corruption of the text, whether as addition or omission, antedates the rise of monasticism. Monks may have favored the copying of "and fasting," but they did not invent the reading.

A possible cause of corruption at Mark 9:29 could be *homeoarchton*, or similar line beginning. We note that the extra words at the end of Mark 9:29 begin with "and" (Καί). Our printed texts begin at Mark 9:30 with the phrase Κἀκεῖθεν. But a number of manuscripts read Καὶ ἐκεῖθεν (ACNW, etc.). If the exemplar available to a very early copyist had this unabbreviated form, there was even greater opportunity for parablepsis. So the omission might have occurred due to the configuration Καὶ . . . Καὶ.[5] The scribe's eye would have dropped from the one Καὶ to the other and missed out a line of ten letters.

This line of argument was thoroughly set forth by A. C. Clark a century ago.[6] Objection has been raised to Clark's work on a number of grounds. In particular it has been noted that Clark's theory requires very narrow columns in some cases (in the case of Mark 9:29 this would mean columns of an average of 10 letters per line). Such narrow columns are exceedingly rare. Metzger notes that this is an argument that has

---

2. France, *Mark*, 361.
3. Metzger, *Textual Commentary*, 85.
4. Metzger and Ehrman, *Text of the New Testament*, 268.
5. Elliott, review of J Harold Greenlee, *The Text of the New Testament*, RBL 01/2009.
6. Clark, *Primitive Text*.

been strengthened by the discovery of a number of early papyri with relatively wide columns.[7] This is undoubtedly the impression gained from a cursory glance at the photographs and transcriptions of P[45], P[66], P[75], etc. But it is far from universal. Several early papyri display narrow columns, for example, P[78] (possibly an amulet), P[113] (11 letters per line), and P. Antinoopolis 2.54, a third century fragment of Matt 6:10–12 has 5–6 letters per line. P[95] is probably another example.[8] These examples are sufficient to show that while 10 letters per line is unusual in New Testament papyri, it is not unknown. And it only takes one early copy to be misread in this way to distort a whole stream of the tradition. It is noteworthy that A. C. Clark theorized that the exemplars of both Codex Sinaiticus and Codex Vaticanus probably contained 10 to 12 letters per line.[9]

Any study of the text of Mark 9:29 must consider the parallel textual question at Matt 17:21. The verse, which is not printed in modern editions, is missing in ℵ* B etc. but is found in C D and in many manuscripts, versions, and early Christian writers including Origen. Interestingly no manuscripts bear witness to the verse in the shorter version as found in ℵ* B k in Mark, without the reference to fasting. Had Matthew copied Mark when his gospel contained only the shorter form, it is likely that some trace of this reading would have survived in the manuscript tradition of Matt. Of course, those who believe that the line was added to the text of Matt will find no difficulty here. But if, as Metzger suggests, the material was derived from Mark and that here "most manuscripts have been assimilated to the parallel in Mark 9:29,"[10] that assimilation must have occurred prior to the mid third century, i.e., before the time of Origen.

## INTERNAL CONSIDERATIONS

When we turn to the matter of the style, theology and literary art of the Gospel of Mark in assessing whether "and fasting" at 9:29 would be consistent with what we find elsewhere in this Gospel we are not disappointed. In particular, the question of fasting receives special attention

---

7. Metzger and Ehrman, *Text of the New Testament*, 213.
8. Comfort and Barrett, *The Text*, 627.
9. Clark, *Primitive Text*, 21, 24, 33.
10. Metzger, *Textual Commentary*, 35.

in Mark 2:18–22, a passage Mark shares with Matthew and Luke. There the question is raised as to why the disciples of Jesus do not fast, whereas the disciples of John and of the Pharisees do. To answer the question, Jesus tells two short parables, one about the bridegroom, and the other about the wine in wineskins. In Mark 2, in speaking of fasting, Jesus uses figurative language, and this will prove significant for our consideration of the text of Mark 9:29. It is also noteworthy that Jesus remarks at the end of the parable, "The days will come when the bridegroom is taken away from them, and then they will fast on that day" (Mark 2:20). We shall return to this comment in our discussion of narrative features affecting the text of Mark 9:29. It is sufficient here to observe that this is the first clear reference to Jesus' death in Mark. James Edwards notes that this is the first of many reminiscences and allusions to Isaiah's Servant of the Lord. "Mark intimates that Jesus, too, will be 'Cut off from the Land of the Living' (Isa. 53:8)."[11] At least we may say that the inclusion of "and fasting" is consistent with Mark's gospel and that we should be alert to the probability that if the words are to be included in the gospel, they are likely to be "figurative" rather than literal.

## NARRATIVE FEATURES

Contemporary studies of miracles in the gospels have exhibited a growing sensitivity to their figurative and symbolic significance, and their importance for Jesus' proclamation of the Kingdom. This has especially been the case in Mark, whose gospel is the work of an accomplished storyteller. Indeed, in recent years there has been a growing appreciation of the narrative features of Mark's gospel. This is true in both senses in which the term *narrative* is used in biblical studies: Mark as storyteller and the stories that shape the narrative.

First, Mark as storyteller. Although Mark's style and language is colloquial and not polished,[12] this writer's narrative technique is far from simplistic.[13] One aspect of Mark's narrative art that is relevant to the present study is the so-called "sandwich technique" in Mark. Mark often inserts a passage into the middle of another story, and the inserted element, the central element, offers a theological or narrative key to the

---

11. Edwards, *Mark*, 91.
12. Elliott, *Language and Style*.
13. Rhoads, Dewey, Michie, *Mark as Story*, 24, 33.

matter on either side of it.[14] It is worthy of note that the story of the boy with the spirit (Mark 9:14–29) exhibits this feature. Just before and just after the story there is a prediction of the passion, (9:12, 9:30–32). It is clear from this feature that the story in 9:14–29 is not an isolated incident of healing, but is connected to the larger story that Mark is telling, with its focus on the death and resurrection of Jesus. We may conclude that the story, and the final saying about prayer (and fasting) must be taken figuratively and not literally. It speaks of more than just heightened spiritual discipline.[15]

The story and saying also takes on new texture if we relate it to the story of God and Israel, which had a formative influence on the Gospel of Mark, indeed, on the whole New Testament. With regard to "prayer and fasting," and my proposal that this is what Mark wrote, it is important to consider the significance of fasting in the Israel of the second temple period. Fasting was expressive of the narrative world of first century Judaism. Among the reasons that the pious Jew fasted in this period was that fasting was a mark of Israel's continuing exile.[16] Zechariah 8:19 lists four fasts, taking place in the fourth, fifth, seventh, and tenth months. N. T. Wright notes, "All four were in fact linked to events connected with the destruction of Jerusalem by the Babylonians; keeping them was a reminder that Israel was still waiting for her real redemption from exile."[17] Of course, the Jews did return from exile, and the temple was rebuilt, but Jews felt, especially in the face of Roman occupation, that they were still in exile. Many were fasting and praying, and like Simeon, "looking forward to the consolation of Israel" (Luke 2:25). I believe that against this background of the sense of ongoing exile in the time of Jesus, the expression "prayer and fasting," and its link with the preceding story, gives new material for assessing the textual question in Mark 9:29. Moreover, I suspect that in the expression "prayer and fasting" we have not a later scribal addition for ascetical motives, but an echo of Dan 9:3. Daniel 9 records the prayer of Daniel concerning the end of the exile in Babylon:

---

14. Edwards, "Markan Sandwiches," 193–216.

15 A defense of the longer reading on grounds that *prayer and fasting* are a symbolic reference to Jesus' death on the cross see Minette de Tillesse, *Le Secret messianique dans*, 98–99.

16 Wright, *The New Testament*, 234–35.

17. Ibid.

> I, Daniel, perceived in the books the number of the years that, according to the word of the Lord to the prophet Jeremiah, must be fulfilled for the devastation of Jerusalem, namely, seventy years. ³ Then I turned to the Lord God, to seek an answer by prayer and supplication with fasting and sackcloth and ashes . . .

In other words, Daniel read the prophecy in Jeremiah 25, and discerned that it was time for the exile to be over. However, Israel was still in exile. It was by prayer and fasting that he sought the Lord to discern what time it was, and when the exile would end in fact.

How does the story of Daniel's prayer and fasting relate to the story of the healing of the boy with the spirit? If we turn back again to Mark 2:18, we read of Jesus and his disciples not fasting, in contrast to the disciples of John and of the Pharisees. This is a clear symbolic indication that with the coming of Jesus, Israel's long exile is finally coming to an end. One sign of the end of exile is the healing ministry of Jesus, not least the healing of the boy. Jesus liberates from the oppression of exile. But the disciples' inability to cast out the spirit is a sign that they did not understand that with Jesus' death and resurrection the exile would be over. Indeed, "They did not understand what he was saying and were afraid to ask him" (9:32). They needed to become like Daniel, and search the scriptures, and pray and fast, asking the question, *What time is it?* Then, like Daniel, they would receive the response. It was precisely in the death and resurrection of Jesus (predicted just before and after this story!) that the Exile would finally come to an end.

The fact that Jesus and his disciples do not fast in Mark 2, but in Mark 9:29 Jesus calls them to "prayer and fasting," appears on the surface to be a contradiction. But it may be Mark's ironic way of stating that whereas in the early days of the ministry the disciples are aware that with the arrival of Jesus the Kingdom of God is breaking in, they fail to understand as the gospel story progresses. Especially after the confession at Caesarea Philippi (8:27–30) when Jesus predicts his death and resurrection as the means whereby he brings about the end of Israel's exile, the disciples manifest a complete misunderstanding. The more Jesus predicts his suffering, the more the disciples miss the point. Such is the irony of Mark's gospel.

If the Marcan Jesus is echoing Daniel 9 and referring to the end of exile, he is participating in a developed tradition of biblical interpretation in ancient Israel. Michael Fishbane has demonstrated that Daniel

9 is itself a re-interpretation and re-contextualization of the old prophecy of Jeremiah 25:9–12. Before Daniel re-interpreted the 70 years of Jeremiah to mean the 70 sabbatical cycles, or 490 years, applying the oracle to the abomination of Antiochus IV Epiphanes and the Maccabean revolt (175–164 BCE) the chronicler had already re-interpreted Jer 25. In 2 Chronicles 36:18–21 the chronicler paved the way for Daniel's re-interpretation by incorporating into his citation of Jeremiah an oracle concerning the jubilee and the land from Lev 26:34–35, "an exegetical revision of significant interest" according to Fishbane.[18] 2 Chronicle 36:19–21 reads: (citation from Lev 26 in italics)

> [19] They burned the house of God, broke down the walls of Jerusalem, burned all the palaces with fire, and destroyed all its precious vessels. [20] He took into exile in Babylon those who had escaped from the sword, and they became servants to him and to his sons until the establishment of the kingdom of Persia. [21] To fulfill the word of the Lord by the mouth of Jeremiah, until *the land had made up for its sabbaths. All the days that it lay desolate it kept sabbath*, to fulfill seventy years.

If Jesus is echoing Daniel 9 in Mark 9:29, he is participating in an developed exegetical tradition in Israel, and using this well established convention of re-contextualizing to declare that in his life, ministry, death and Resurrection the exile is finally over.

Several phrases in the story at Mark 9:14–29, which had puzzled commentators, may be illuminated by the perception that the key question being addressed here is *What time is it?* Twice Jesus asks the question, "How long?" He answered them, "You faithless generation, how much longer must I be among you? How much longer must I put up with you?" (9:19); and, "Jesus asked the father, 'How long has this been happening to him?'" (9:21). The question of time is of critical importance to the story, and was key for any Jew who was longing for the end of the exile.

In addition, Jesus' reference to the "faithless generation" in Mark 9:19 points to a wider narrative focus of the story. This reference is neither to the disciples, nor the crowd, nor the father, but is aimed at "the whole people and not at individuals."[19] Most commentators note a possible echo of Deut 32:5, "a prophetic grievance against unbelieving

---

18. Fishbane, *Biblical Interpretation in Ancient Israel*, 481.
19. Büchsel, γενεά, κτλ, *TDNT* I, 663.

Israel."[20] In this story Jesus is painting on a wider canvass, telling the larger story of God and his people. For this is the *Song of Moses*, well known and much studied in the time of Jesus.[21] That song laments:

> Yet his degenerate children have dealt falsely with him, a perverse and crooked generation. (Deut 32:5)

> . . . for they are a perverse generation children in whom there is no faithfulness. (Deut 32:20)

Wright's perceptive work on the importance of ongoing exile for understanding the story of Jesus in the gospels has been much studied and debated.[22] Brant Pitre has conducted an extensive study of the Jewish sense of ongoing exile in the period, and offered the refinement that such a perception was as great, if not greater, among people from the northern tribes who never experienced the return from exile as did the people of Jerusalem, who had been taken off to Babylon and returned under Cyrus. Pitre makes the important observation that "*There was not one exile in Israel's history but two.* For long before the Babylonian Exile of the two southern tribes of Judah took place in 586 (2 Kings 24–25) the ten northern tribes of Israel had been scattered among the Gentiles in the Assyrian Exile of 722 BCE (2 Kings 15–17)."[23] This refinement of the sense of ongoing exile, and longing for its end in second temple Judaism has a bearing on my proposal regarding "prayer and fasting" as expressive of a longing for the end of the Exile. The incident of the transfiguration and the healing that followed it took place in the territory of the former Northern Kingdom, whether the setting of the story was at Mount Tabor or further north at Mount Hermon. The sense of ongoing exile would have been especially poignant to Jews living in "Galilee of the Gentiles."

---

20. Edwards, *Mark*, 278

21. See 4 Mac. 18:18-19. For a fascinating discussion of exegetical interest in Deut 32, traceable to the second temple period see Tov, "The Septuagint as a Source for the Literary Analysis of the Hebrew Scripture," in Evans and Tov, *Exploring the Origins* 41–43.

22. Pitre, *Jesus, the Tribulation*, 31.

23. Ibid., 33–34, italics original.

## TRANSMISSION HISTORY

From the preceding proposal it may be possible to suggest a history of the transmission of the text of Mark 9:29. Mark originally wrote "prayer and fasting," which would have been understood as an echo of Dan 9:3, a code for the sense of ongoing exile in Israel, and a challenge to understand what time it was, i.e., time for the exile to end. Matthew took over this form of the saying in his own record of the incident at Matt 17:21, and this form survives in some manuscripts of Matt. Early on a scribe of Mark made the mistake of jumping from the Καὶ of one line to its occurrence in the next, and so lost ten letters. The text makes good sense in the shorter form. And its narrative and theological significance will have been missed especially by copyists of a gentile background, who did not share the sense of continuing exile that was so fundamental to the thinking of second temple Jews, especially in the territories of the old Northern Kingdom. Nevertheless, the words have survived in the vast majority of the New Testament manuscript tradition and should be printed in our modern editions and translations.

# 10

## Luke 4:18[1]

THE KING JAMES TRANSLATION of Luke 4:18 includes the phrase "to heal the brokenhearted" in the long quotation from Isaiah 61 in Jesus speech in the synagogue at Nazareth. The phrase is missing from the modern editions and translations of the New Testament. In this essay I will argue that it is part of the original text of the gospel, and that it is important to the theology of Luke, and vital for our understanding of the healing power of the Christian faith.

### TWO REJECTIONS

Luke 4:16–30 is the story of Jesus' preaching and rejection in the synagogue in Nazareth. He read from the prophet Isaiah chapter 61, adding words from Isa 58:6. He followed the reading with the comment, "Today this scripture has been fulfilled in your hearing." The positive response to a local boy with a growing ministry turned negative as Jesus continued to expound with proverbs and stories from the scriptures.

> Doubtless you will quote to me this proverb, "Doctor, cure yourself!" And you will say, "Do here also in your hometown the things we have heard you did at Capernaum." And he said, "Truly I tell you, no prophet is acceptable in the prophet's home town."

The reaction went from bad to worse as Jesus gave famous examples from the ministries of Elijah and Elisha of healings outside of Israel, the widow of Zerapath and Naaman the Syrian. The audience reacted violently and sought to kill Jesus. Jesus was rejected at Nazareth.

---

1. This chapter appeared earlier in Ellens, *The Healing Power of Spirituality*. Vol. 1, 162–69 and is reproduce with kind permission of ABC-CLIO.

But in the story of Jesus' rejection in his hometown is another tale of rejection. One of the key elements in the quotation is from Isa 61 in Luke 4:18, the phrase "to heal the brokenhearted." This phrase is rejected by modern editors of the text of the New Testament. Editors and commentators would concur with the UBS committee, who judged the words to be "an obvious scribal supplement introduced in order to bring the quotation more completely in accord with the Septuagint text of Isa 61:1."[2] They are not found in what are generally considered the "oldest and best" manuscripts of the New Testament (ℵ B D etc.). Concerning the textual variation J. A. Fitzmyer writes, "the omission . . . is of little consequence."[3] The essay that follows questions both parts of this assertion. Has Luke omitted the phrase? Is the notice about the healing of the brokenhearted of little consequence?

New Testament textual critics take various different factors into consideration in making a judgment concerning which readings are what the author originally wrote. In addition to the external manuscript support for any reading, there are internal factors like the theology and style of the author. In addition both intrinsic and transcriptional probabilities must be weighed. We will consider each of these factors in putting the case for the originality of the longer text at Luke 4:18. Final decision as to the original text requires the critic to be both scientist and artist.

## MANUSCRIPT SUPPORT

Modern students of the text point out that the extra line from Luke 4:18 is not found in the oldest manuscripts of Luke. A few scholars believe that it is original with Luke.[4] The reading is found in a large number of manuscripts, versions and in several early Christian writers.

It is worthy of note that among the witnesses for the longer reading is Irenaeus.[5] We note that in *Against Heresies* IV.xiii.1 Irenaeus is not quoting from Isaiah 61, but consciously referring to Luke 4. It appears, therefore, that he is not harmonizing to the LXX, but citing what he

---

2. Metzger, *Textual Commentary*, 114.

3. Fitzmyer, *Luke I–IX*, 532. The majority of scholars concur in this judgment. However, a few have argued that the line is original with Luke, Grundmann, *Lukas*, 118; H Schürmann, *Das Lukasevangelium*, 229 n. 58.

4. Grundmann, *Lukas*, 118, Schürmann, *Lukasevangelium*, I, 229.

5. Sanday and Turner, *Novum Testamentum Sancti Irenii*. 55.

finds in the text of Luke. It is not always easy to weigh the value of patristic quotations, but this citation from the late second century bishop of Lyons in Gaul, if authentic, would constitute our earliest witness to the verse in the manuscript tradition. At the very least we may say that the longer reading was current in the so-called "western" tradition in the second century.

There has been a growing appreciation in text-critical circles for the value of patristic evidence. For example, Bart Ehrman, in his study of the text of Luke 3:22 notes the value of the testimony of Justin Martyr, Clement of Alexandria, and the *Gospel According to the Hebrews* in witnessing to a reading *earlier* than that found in $P^4$ or the great uncials (ℵ B D), the manuscripts normally given greater weight in decisions on the text.[6] It is therefore no longer sufficient to dismiss a reading simply by noting that it is not found in the "earliest and best" manuscripts. A fresh assessment of the external evidence is called for.

## TRANSCRIPTIONAL PROBABILITIES

In Tischendorf's eighth edition of the Greek New Testament the presentation of evidence for the longer reading at Luke 4:18 is followed by the succinct "e LXX" (i.e., from the Septuagint). Most scholars, together with the *Textual Commentary*, adopt this explanation, that the words were added to conform to the LXX. Bruce Metzger notes, "since monks knew by heart extensive portions of the scriptures, the temptation to harmonize discordant parallels or quotations would be strong in proportion to the copyist's familiarity with other parts of the Bible."[7] But for the present case, the evidence from Irenaeus comes from before the rise of monasticism. Moreover, the argument for "harmonization" especially in the gospel tradition has recently been called into question.[8] Fresh scrutiny must also be given to the assumption of harmonization in the case of Old Testament quotations.

On the other hand, the possibility of accidental omission by scribes of Luke's gospel has become more attractive in recent years. Whereas earlier studies had emphasized the tendency of scribes to *add* to their manuscripts, several scholars working on the early papyri have shown

---

6. Ehrman, *Orthodox Corruption*, 62.
7. Metzger and Ehrman, *Text of the New Testament*, 262.
8. Michael W. Holmes, "Text of the Matthean Divorce Passages," 651–64.

that the scribes of these manuscripts were more prone to *omit* material as they copied.⁹

## INTERNAL CONSIDERATIONS

When we turn to internal criteria for assessing a textual variation, matters of style, theology and the like, we find that the longer reading is certainly compatible with the Gospel of Luke. We note that the word for healing (ἰάομαι) is common in this gospel. Indeed, Luke is by far the most frequent user of this Greek verb. The figures from Moulton and Geden are as follows: Luke 11; Matthew 4; Acts 4; John 3; Mark 1; Hebrews 1; James 1; 1 Peter 1. Furthermore, that healing is an important emphasis in the Gospel of Luke is undeniable, whatever weight we may give to the tradition that the author was "the beloved physician" (Col 4:14).

Joel B. Green asks pointedly why either Jesus or Luke would have dropped this phrase from Isa 61:1.¹⁰ A number of suggestions have been made. Reviewing the possibilities (An attempt to avoid connecting Jesus' miraculous healings with the Spirit? Concentration on messianic interpretation?) F. Bovon concludes, "neither is convincing, but I have no better suggestion."¹¹ But no further suggestion is needed if Luke included the line from Isa 61 in his gospel.

Attempts have been made to settle the question of the text of Luke 4:18 on literary and stylistic grounds. In a recent discussion of the story of the rejection at Nazareth, Kenneth E. Bailey has argued that the whole passage, with the encasing of Isa 61:1-2 in the center, conforms to a carefully framed rhetorical structure. According to Bailey, the omission of the phrase "to bind up the brokenhearted" is important (together with an addition from Isa 58:6) to maintain that rhetorical structure.¹² At first sight his presentation seems quite convincing. But in an earlier study Bo Reicke argued that the rhetorical structure calls for the inclusion of the

---

9. Royce, *Scribal Habits*, Head, "Observations," 240–47, and "Habits of New Testament Copyists," 399–408.

10. Green, *Luke*, 206.

11. Bovon, *Luke 1*, 153.

12. Bailey, *Jesus Through Middle Eastern Eyes*, 149. Despite my disagreement with Bailey on the text, I find his treatment of the passage penetrating and compelling in other respects.

line from Isa 61:1c.[13] Arguments from chiasm and other literary patterns are seemingly inconclusive in solving the text-critical question.

## NARRATIVE FEATURES

Every culture has a story to tell, and every group within that culture has its own peculiar telling of the common story.[14] Often the specific understanding of the common story by a subgroup will find expression in the way that group imagines the story to end, and their own place in that climax. So it is with Judaism in the second temple period. All groups shared the same story: Creation and covenant, exodus and exile, kingdom and messiah. But each told the story, especially the final chapter in their own way. For the people of Israel that story was told using midrashic methods, the re-telling and interpreting of scripture. Therefore, by comparing and contrasting midrashic methods of the different groups, we may bring into sharper focus the distinctive self-understanding and theology of each.

The pioneering analysis of this story from the standpoint of comparative midrash was written by J. A. Sanders in 1975.[15] Sanders compared and contrasted the use of Isa 61:1-2 in the Qumran document 11QMelch and Luke 4:16-30. Both texts make extensive use of Isa 61. For the fragment from the Dead Sea Scrolls, words and phrases from the Isaiah text appear in lines 4, 6, 13, 14, and 18-20.[16] Luke represents Jesus reading the first two verses of Isa 61 in the context of a synagogue homily in his home town. Both texts link Isaiah 61 to the Year of Jubilee in Leviticus 25, but whereas the link is explicit in Qumran, it is implicit in Luke 4.[17]

The linking of two or more biblical passages together because of similar words, phrases, or ideas is the Jewish interpretive technique called *gezerah shewah*. This literally means "an equivalent regulation,"

---

13. Reicke, "Jesus in Nazareth," 47–55.

14. See Wright, *The New Testament*," 6–144.

15. Sanders, "From Isaiah 61 to Luke 4," 75–106; rev. in Sanders and Evans, *Luke and Scripture*, 46–69.

16. Sanders cites this observation originally made by Miller in "The Function of Isaiah 61:1-2," 647–69. The text of 11Q Melch is found in Vermes, *The Dead Sea Scrolls in English*, 532–34.

17. For the idea of Jubilee in Luke 4 see Bovon, *Luke 1*, 154, and many other commentators.

and was one of the seven exegetical rules of Hillel the Elder. The rule states that one passage of scripture may be explained by another if similar words or phrases are present.[18] The use of this technique is evident in the Nazareth periscope in Luke 4. Several passages have been brought together and illuminate each other because of a similar word, phrase or idea. Scholars have generally recognized this, but have offered various suggestions concerning the catchword that brought the passages together. Perhaps it was the word "acceptable" (δεκτόν).[19] Some have suggested that the link word was "forgiveness" or "release" (ἄφεσιν), a word found in both Isa 61:1–2 and Isa 58:6.[20] There may also be a link based on a parallel between Sabbath and Jubilee.[21] However, there is another word and theme that may tie together all the elements found in Jesus' synagogue homily in Luke 4:16–30. That word is "healing." If the line in question, "to heal the brokenhearted," is restored to the text in Luke 4:18, a verbal link is established with the proverb of verse 23, "Doctor, cure yourself." There is also, of course, the conceptual link with the two Old Testament stories of Elijah (vv. 25–26) and Elijah (v. 27). In other words, restore the missing words in v. 18 and the whole passage makes perfect sense from the standpoint of Jewish interpretation.

I conclude that on both external (manuscript) and internal (stylistic and theological) grounds, and especially from the perspective of Jewish narrative technique, the line "to heal the brokenhearted" is not only fitting, but essential to the story of the rejection of Jesus at Nazareth.

## CONCLUDING APPLICATION

It is generally recognized that the story of the rejection of Jesus at Nazareth plays a central role in Luke's gospel. Many scholars use the word "programmatic" to describe the function of the episode in Luke. Richard Hays, for example, wrote that by placing the synagogue episode at the beginning, Luke "turned it into a programmatic statement."[22] David Balch suggested recently, "The sermon supplies the basic themes for the whole two volume history."[23] Other scholars have noted the im-

---

18. Evans, "Jewish Exegesis," in *DTIB*, 382.
19. Bovon, *Luke 1*, 153.
20. Fitzmyer, *Luke I-IX*, 533.
21. Bock, *Luke 1:1—9:50*, 405
22. Hays, *Moral Vision*, 115.
23. Balch in Dunn and Rogerson, *Commentary on the Bible*, 112–13.

portance of the story and its implications for politics[24] and mission.[25] Indeed, Christopher J. H. Wright is not wide of the mark to state that Jesus' quotation from Isa 61 is "the clearest programmatic statement" of the inbreaking of the eschatological reign of God.[26]

If the mission of Jesus includes the healing of the brokenhearted, and the words from Isa 61:1 belong in the original text of Luke's gospel, there are important implications for our application of the gospel in the world today. We may ask, what is the importance of Jesus including this line, "to heal the brokenhearted," as the first item in his proclamation of the kingdom of God?

To answer this question we need to consider the radical nature of Jesus' teaching both for his contemporary culture and for the twenty-first century world. In his article on "comparative midrash" James A. Sanders drew a contrast between the teaching of Qumran (11Q Melch) and Jesus (Luke 4). Qumran and Jesus had much in common. In particular, both the Essenes and Jesus believed that they were living in the end time, and that the scripture was being fulfilled in their day. Just as the Qumran applied the scriptures to their own community, so Jesus states, "Today this scripture has been fulfilled in your hearing"(Luke 4:21). But where they differed was in their attitude towards their enemies. On this point Sanders writes:

> Where they differ radically is in the Lucan Jesus' midrash on who the poor, the captives and the blind were. Whereas 11QMelch, by citing Lev 25:10 and Isa.52:7, reflects the second Essene axiom that the captives to be released are the in-group of the Essenes, Jesus' citation of the gracious acts of Elijah and Elisha toward the Sidonian widow and the Syrian leper shows that he does not subscribe to the Essene second Axiom.[27]

In other words, whereas Qumran (and Jesus' listeners at Nazareth) expected blessing for the insider and "the day of vengeance of our God" (Isa 61:2) for the outsider, Jesus offered the blessings of release and healing to the outsider. This is reflected in the radical teaching of Jesus, "Love your enemies and do good to those who hate you, bless those who curse you, pray for those who abuse you" (Luke 6:27–28) and the remarkable

---

24. Yoder, *The Politics of Jesus*, 34–40.
25. Wright, *ABD*, 3:1025–30.
26. Wright, *The Mission of God*, 309.
27. Sanders, "From Isaiah 61 to Luke 4," 62.

action of Jesus, "Father, forgive them, for they do not know what they are doing." (Luke 23:34). The healing of the brokenhearted consisted not only in the reversal of their fortunes, but in their ability to find freedom and cleansing by forgiving their enemies. Herein lies the radical nature of the good news of Jesus Christ for his day and for our own.

In his landmark discussion of the gospel of reconciliation, *Exclusion and Embrace*, Miroslav Volf explores the nature of this healing of the brokenhearted as it applies to our contemporary, war-torn world. This study, born out of the conflicts in Volf's native land, the former Yugoslavia, points to the necessity of change not only in the heart of the oppressor, but in the heart of the oppressed. Both need to repent. In a section entitled "The Politics of the Pure Heart," Volf writes, commenting on Luke 4:16–30,

> The truly revolutionary character of Jesus' proclamation lies precisely in the *connection between the hope he gives to the oppressed and the radical change he requires of them.*[28]

The poor and oppressed are not healed of their broken hearts simply by the reversal of fortunes. Those who have lost their families in war or their homes or jobs in recession, their innocence to abuse, their reputation to slander, or their clean air to polluters are not healed simply by seeing themselves vindicated or reimbursed and their enemies punished. A radical healing of the broken heart is required, and this can only come by repentance of the hatred and envy which the circumstances of oppression have allowed to gain a foothold. Such radical repentance is not easy. In many cases in our war-torn world it seems impossible. But with Jesus as mentor, model and mediator it is possible. Through his proclamation, his life, his death and his resurrection, and the new kingdom of freedom and reconciliation there is the opportunity for the healing of the brokenhearted.

---

28. Volf, *Exclusion and Embrace*, 114.

# Conclusion

THE PRECEDING STUDIES ARE an experiment in New Testament Textual Criticism. The aim has been to explore the narrative features of verses within the New Testament, indicated by a quotation, allusion or echo of the Old Testament, and thereby to bring fresh material and perspective to bear upon the textual problems within these verses. This conclusion draws some implications from this study for the areas of textual criticism, exegesis and theology.

## TEXTUAL CRITICISM

The text-critical decisions proposed in these chapters have been reached using an eclectic method, with some surprising and even radical results. But none of these proposals is without support in modern scholarly discussion. In three of the verses reviewed in this book the study of narrative features adds further support to the decision of the editors of UBS[4]/Nestle[27] (Luke 3:22; Luke 22:43–44; Acts 20:28). Three of the readings I defend as original are supported by the earliest available manuscripts (Rom 8:28; Luke 3:22; Acts 20:28). For the other seven I advance reasons for considering as original readings that are not supported by what are commonly deemed the "oldest and best witnesses." Three readings are supported by the majority of witnesses (Luke 3:22; Mark 9:29; Luke 4:18). And yet, I defend as original several readings that have slender support in the manuscript tradition (Heb 2:9; Mark 15:34; Phil 4:7). But even this fact should not automatically disqualify them as later alterations of the original text. Our standard critical editions accept a number of readings as original that have similar slender attestation. Clearly we cannot simply follow one standard, and choose either the oldest, the "best," or the greatest number of manuscripts. The whole range of external evidence needs to be considered. Sometimes, as Ehrman has demonstrated in the case of Heb 2:9, the crucial evidence may be found in minuscules or patristic citations.[1]

Textual critics customarily follow certain rules in assessing the merits of variant readings and making textual decisions.[2] This book scrutinizes three of these rules: 1) The shorter reading is to be preferred, 2) The more difficult reading is to be preferred, and 3) The reading that differs from a parallel in the Old Testament or the New Testament is more likely to be original (harmonization).

## The Shorter Reading

*The Shorter reading is to be preferred* (*lectio brevior potior*). The logic of this rule is that scribes tended to add to the manuscripts as they copied to explain, clarify or correct the texts they were copying. But serious questions have been raised in recent years concerning the application of this rule. James Royse's study of the early New Testament papyri has demonstrated that the earliest copyists were more prone to omit from their texts than to add to them.[3] Similar developments have occurred in the textual criticism of the Old Testament. Emanuel Tov has noted instances where the longer reading in the textual tradition of the Hebrew Bible is likely the original one. Tov concludes concerning *lectio brevior*:

> The validity of this rule cannot be maintained in all instances. In fact, neither in the NT nor in the Hebrew Bible can it be decided automatically that the shorter reading is original.[4]

This methodological development has aided in the explorations of several of the textual variations in this book: five of the ten essays have argued for the originality of the longer reading: Rom 8:28; Luke 22:43–44; Phil 4:7; Mark 9:29; Luke 4:18. In Phil 4:7 and Mark 9:29 the phenomenon of *homeotes* (similarity of letters) likely accounts for a scribe's inadvertent deletion.

---

1. Ehrman, *Orthodox Corruption*, 146.
2. Metzger and Ehrman, *Text of the New Testament*, 300–305.
3. Royse, *Scribal Habits*.
4. Tov, *Textual Criticism of the Hebrew Bible*, 306.

## The More Difficult Reading

*The more difficult reading is to be preferred (lectio difficilior praeferenda).* According to this canon of textual criticism the reading is to be preferred as original that is judged to be more difficult and, therefore, subject to change by later scribes. Tov also raises questions about the application of this rule to textual criticism. He warns that "what appears as a linguistically or textually difficult reading to one scholar may not necessarily be difficult to another."[5] This caution corresponds to the judgment of the Alands concerning the rule *lectio difficilior preferanda* that this principle must not be applied too mechanically.[6] An example of the difficulty of applying this rule emerges from or study of Mark 15:34. Undoubtedly, the reading "why have you persecuted me?" in Jesus' cry from the cross would have struck some scribes as problematic. It is clearly the more difficult reading. Nevertheless, most modern critics have deemed it too difficult, and condemned it on external grounds. However, if we consider that Mark has here followed the exegetical practice of merging two texts (in this case Psalm 22 and Psalm 69) the phraseology "why have you persecuted me?" no longer seems impossibly problematic. Similarly, if the story of Psalm 22 is perceived to stand behind Hebrews 2, then the reading "apart from God" becomes less difficult. Scribes who could no longer hear Psalm 22 in Hebrews 2 found the expression troublesome and made the change to the more common "by the grace of God." The question of the more difficult reading is also relevant to the text of Acts 20:28. The expression "the church of God that he purchased with his own blood," understandably difficult for later scribes, is reasonable when understood in the context of the three Old Testament texts echoed in Paul's speech to the Ephesian elders. What has happened is that the texts containing these readings have moved from a culture that understood the Jewish story, techniques and assumptions into a Gentile culture where they were not understood.[7]

---

5. Ibid., 304.

6. Aland and Aland, *Text of the New Testament*, 276.

7. See Walls, *Mission Movement*, 16–18. It is significant that Walls was a New Testament textual critic before he became a mission historian.

## Harmonization

The assumption among textual critics that scribes often harmonized or assimilated the manuscripts they were copying to a more familiar text in the Old or New Testament has also featured in our study. Clearly the pressure to harmonize would be great at Mark 15:34, where the scribe would seek to conform the reading either to Ps 22:1 or to Matt 27:46. But other cases are more problematic. Did scribes copying Luke 3:22, either accidentally or intentionally, conform their texts to Ps 2:7 or to the synoptic parallels (Matt 3:17, Mark 1:11)? A careful review of arguments from assimilation will give special attention to those New Testament passages that have resisted harmonization. Why, for example, do we not find among the variants at 1 Pet 3:15 listed in the *Edition Critica Maior* any traces of the form found in our printed texts of the LXX? Why are there no manuscripts that omit the exceptive clause in Matthew 5:32? Why is there no trace of the shorter reading fom Mark 9:29 at Matthew 17:21? A starting point for pursuing the question of harmonization should be Michael Holmes' study of the divorce sayings in the gospels and D. C. Parker's valuable review of the issue.[8]

## EXEGESIS

In the past it was assumed that Textual Criticism, sometimes called "lower criticism," was to perform the humble task of establishing the text with which others would do exegesis, theology and ethics. But this is no longer the case. Textual criticism and exegesis are interrelated. The study of intertextuality is a contributor to this shift. Texts from the Old Testament quoted or alluded to in New Testament passages have played an important role in the establishing of the New Testament text. This has been the case in the echoes of single passages at Rom 8:28; Heb 2:9; Phil 4:7; Rom 8:2; and Mark 9:29. Other New Testament verses involving textual questions cite Old Testament texts in combination. In our study these include Luke 3:22; Mark 15:34; Luke 22:43–44; Acts 20:28; and Luke 4:18. Placing these Old Testament references in the foreground and exploring their exegetical significance offers new material and perspective for the solution of textual problems. The narratives indicated by these texts of the Old Testament are critical not only for exegesis but for textual criticism. Thus Gen 50:20, and the story of Joseph, not only pro-

---

8. Holmes, "The Text," 651–64; Parker, *Introduction*, 338–41.

vides a pattern for Paul's exploration of God's restoration of his people in Romans 9–11, but also assists in the solution of the textual problem at Rom 8:28. The combination of Old Testament texts in the voice at the baptism of Jesus both offers avenues for exploring the meaning of Jesus' Baptism, and also indicates the solution to the textual issue at Luke 3:22. The three Old Testament texts alluded to in Acts 20:28 may constitute both the exegetical key to Paul's speech at Ephesus, but also the solution to the textual issues in the passage. The exegete who hears the echo of Psalm 22 in Heb 2:9, or Psalm 130 in Rom 8:2, or Dan 9:3 in Mark 9:29 finds unexpected help with the textual issues in these verses. Textual criticism and exegesis have been described as "siamese twins."[9] They cannot and should not be separated. And the exploration of the intertextual texture of the New Testament documents proves very fruitful.

## THEOLOGY

Long ago C. H. Dodd referred to the use of the Old Testament in the New Testament as "the substructure of New Testament theology."[10] The studies that followed Dodd's pioneering work underline how vital is the task of exploring scriptural intertextuality for theological formulation. All subsequent Christian theology developed from these beginnings. But textual criticism and theology have often operated in separate worlds, each taking little notice of the other. This situation is now changing, due in part to the contribution of Epp, Ehrman, and Parker in showing that a number of textual variations in the New Testament are evidence of early theological discussion. Challenged by their proposals, I turned afresh the study of textual variations within quotations of the Old Testament in the New Testament. I also included the allusions and echoes of scripture, to which increasing attention has been given since the publication of Richard Hays' *Echoes of Scripture in the Letters of Paul*. This avenue of investigation has shown that the context of second temple Judaism is equally as fruitful as the Christological debates of the second and third centuries for explaining textual change. I found that the study of New Testament variations within citations from the scriptures of Israel provided a useful point of departure for the practice of textual criticism with a theological focus. Thus I came to see the textual critic as a full

---

9. Parker, *Introduction*, 183, credits J. Delobel with the remark.
10. The subtitle of his *According to the Scriptures*, 1952.

partner in the interpretive task. This particular class of variations offers some of the earliest and best data for the theological interpretation of Scripture.[11]

And this earliest Christian theology is itself a participant in the developing Jewish exegesis of scripture out of which it grew. The Jewish character of New Testament exegesis has not always been appreciated. It is within the narrative world expressed in Jewish scripture interpretation that the New Testament writings had their origin. Thus the New Testament authors became part of a conversation that was already in progress. They have their distinctive way of telling the Jewish story, but in so doing they fully share the techniques and assumptions of their contemporaries within Judaism. The conviction that the time of fulfillment is at hand, and the creative combination of scripture texts to express this conviction are examples of shared assumptions and techniques. The particulars of an Old Testament quotation (form, introduction, selection, application, history and function) are most fruitfully studied in this Jewish context. This comparative exegesis will reveal both what is shared among the groups in Judaism and what is unique to the Christian telling of the story of God and his people. It brings into sharp focus the Christian claim that the Jewish story reached its climax in the life, death, resurrection, exaltation and new community of Jesus the Messiah.

---

11. Rodgers, "Textual Criticism," 784–87.

# Appendix

Variants adopted by UBS³ with no support from the papyri or the great uncials. Reprinted with permission from *Novum Testamentum* 34 (1992) 391. (// = all manuscripts listed in UBS³.)

| Relevant witnesses | | |
|---|---|---|
| (01 B) | Matt. 3:16 | αὐτῷ 01ᵇ C Dˢᵘᵖᵖ K L P W Δ |
| (01 B) | Matt. 6:33 | τὴν βασιλείαν τοῦ θεοῦ καὶ τὴν δικαιοσύνην αὐτοῦ K L W |
| (01 B) | Matt. 7:14 | τί 01ᶜ1 B³ τί δέ C K L W Xᵒʳⁱᵈ Δ Θ Π $f^1$ $f^{13}$ 28 |
| (01 B) | Matt. 7:18 | ποιεῖν...ποιεῖν 01 C K L W X Δ |
| (01 B) | Matt. 8:9 | ὑπὸ ἐξουσίαν C K L W |
| (01 B) | Matt. 8:21 | τῶν μαθητῶν αὐτοῦ C K L W |
| (01 BD) | Matt. 15:14 | τυφλοί εἰσιν ὁδηγοί τυφλῶν 01ᵃ L Θ $f^{13}$ 33 |
| (01 BD) | Matt. 15:31 | λαλοῦντας, κυλλοὺς ὑγιεῖς C K L P W |
| (01 BD) | Matt. 16:21 | ὁ Ἰησοῦς 01ᵇ C /B³ Δ *omit* ὁ K L W N Δ Θ |
| (P⁴⁵ 01 BD) | Matt. 20:30 | ἐλέησον ἡμᾶς, κύριε p¹⁵ ʳⁱᵈ C K W X Γ |
| (01 BD) | Matt. 23:26 | τοῦ ποτηρίου...τὸ ἐκτὸς αὐτοῦ Θ $f^1$ 700 itᵃ, ᵒ syrᵃ geo¹, ᴬ // |
| (01 ABD) | Matt. 27:16 | Ἰησοῦν Βαραββᾶν Θ $f^1$ 700* syr².ᵖᵃˡᵐˢˢ arm geo² Origen |
| (01 ABD) | Matt. 27:17 | Ἰησοῦν τὸν Βαραββᾶν (Θ 700* omit τόν $f^1$ syrˢ·ᵖᵃˡ arm geo² Origenᵖᵗ // |
| (01 ABD) | Mark 4:20 | Λευί C (01ᶜ B L W Λευείν) $f^1$ 700 |
| (01 ABD) | Mark 4:20 | ἐν...ἐν...ἐν (L ἐν...ἐν...ἐν) Θ Lcct itᵃᵘʳ, ⁽ᵇ⁾,ᶜ,ᵈ,ᵉ,ˡ,ff²,ⁱ,ˡ,q,ʳ¹ vg copˢᵃ,ᵇᵒ goth geo // |
| (01 ABD) | Mark 12:23 | ἐν τῇ ἀναστάσει ὅταν ἀναστῶσιν X 1010 1195 1242 |
| (01 ABD) | Mark 14:72 | ὅτι πρὶν ἀλέκτορα φωνῆσαι δὶς τρίς με ἀπαρνήσῃ C²ᵛⁱᵈ L Ψ |
| (P⁴⁵ ⁷⁵ 01 AB) | Luke 11:14 | καὶ αὐτὸ ἦν Aᶜ C K W X Δ Θ Π Ψ $f^{13}$ 28 |
| (P⁶⁶ 01 ABD) | John 13:2 | Ἰούδας Σίμωνος Ἰσκαριώτου L Ψ 0124 1241 vgᶜˡ arm Origen // |
| (P⁶⁶ 01 ABD) | John 13:32 | ἐν αὐτῷ 2148 /¹⁸⁴·¹⁸⁵ syrᵖ·ʰ·ᵖᵃˡᵐˢˢ Origen // |
| (01 ABD) | John 16:13 | ὁδηγήσει ὑμᾶς ἐν τῇ ἀληθείᾳ πάσῃ (01ᵃ *omit* πάσῃ) 01*· L W |
| (01 ABD) | Rom. 5:1 | ἔχωμεν 01ᵃ B³ Gᵍʳ P Ψ 0220ᵛⁱᵈ |
| (01 ABD) | Rom. 7:25 | χάρις δὲ τῷ θεῷ 01ᵃ Ψ 33 81 88 104 436 2127 copᵇᵒ arm |
| (P⁴⁶ 01 ABD) | 1 Cor. 5:13 | κρινεῖ B³ 33 81 88 104 181 326 436 614 630 1739 1877 1881 |
| (01 ABD) | Phil. 3:21 | αὐτῷ B³ K 33 88 330 |
| (P⁴⁶ 01 ABD) | Col. 1:7 | ὑμῶν 01ᶜ C Dᶜ K P Ψ 33 88 |
| (P⁹⁶ 01 ABD) | Heb. 5:12 | τινά Ψ 81 copˢᵃᵐˢ Euthalius Ps-Oecumeniusᶜᵒᵐᵐ // |
| (01 AB) | Jas. 3:3 | εἰ δέ B³ L Ψ 049 33 104 181 |
| (01 A) | Jas. 4:14 | ἀτμίς γάρ ἐστε ἡ 81 104 614 2412 2492 syrʰ |
| (01 AB) | 1 John 5:18 | αὐτόν 330 451 614 1505 2412 2495 itᵃʳ,ᶜ,ᵈᵉᵐ·ᵈⁱᵛ·ᵖ,q·ᵗ vg syrʰ copᵇᵒ Chromatius Jerome // |
| (P⁴⁷ 01 A) | Rev. 9:13 | ἐκ τῶν τεσσάρων κεράτων P 046 1 1006 1828 1854 1859 2020 |
| (P⁴⁷ 01 A) | Rev. 15:6 | λίνον Γ 051 1 1006 1611 1859 2020ᵗˣᵗ 2042 2065 |
| (01 A) | Rev. 18:3 | πέπωκαν 1828 // |
| (01 A) | Rev. 18:8 | κύριος ὁ θεός 01ᶜ C P 046 051 1 94 1611 1828 1854 2065 2073 2081 |
| (01 A) | Rev. 19:6 | κύριος ὁ θεὸς ἡμῶν 01ʰ P 046 94 1611 1854 1859 2020 2042 2053 |
| (01 A) | Rev. 19:7 | δώσωμεν P 2081 2344 // |
| (01 A) | Rev. 19:11 | καλούμενος πιστὸς καὶ ἀληθινός 046 94 (1006 καὶ καλούμενος) |
| (01 A) | Rev. 21:4 | ὅτι τὰ πρῶτα 01ᵃ 046 1 1854 1859 2020 2081 2138 itᵃʳ,ᵈᵉᵐ vg syrᵇ |

# Bibliography

Aland, K., and B. Aland. *The Text of the New Testament: An Introduction to the Critical Editions and to the Theory and Practice of Modern Textual Criticism.* Grand Rapids: Eerdmans, 1989.
Alter, R. *The Book of Psalms: A Translation with Commentary.* New York: Norton, 2007.
Attridge, H. W. *A Commentary on the Epistle to the Hebrews.* Hermeneia. Philadelphia: Fortress, 1989.
Bailey, K. E. *Jesus through Middle Eastern Eyes: Cultural Studies in the Gospels.* Downers Grove, IL: InterVarsity, 2008.
Balch, D. "Luke." In *Eerdmans Commentary on the Bible*, edited by J. D. G. Dunn and J. W. Rogerson, 1104–60. Grand Rapids: Eerdmans, 2003.
Barrett, C. K. *A Commentary on the Epistle to the Romans.* New York: Harper, 1957.
Bauckham, R. *Jesus and the Eyewitnesses: The Gospels as Eyewitness Testimony.* Grand Rapids: Eerdmans, 2006.
———. "Reading Scripture as a Coherent Story." In *The Art of Reading Scripture*, edited by E. F. Davis and R. B. Hays, 38–53.Grand Rapids: Eerdmans, 2003.
Beale, G. K. and Carson, D. A. *Commentary on the New Testament Use of the Old Testament.* Grand Rapids: Baker Academic, 2007.
Bellinger, W. H., and W. R. Farmer. *Jesus and the Suffering Servant: Isaiah 53 and Christian Origins.* Harrisburg, PA: Trinity, 1998.
Bengel, J. A. *Gnomon of the New Testament.* Edited by C. T. Lewis and M. R. Vincent. Philadelphia: Perkinpine & Higgins, 1864.
Bird, M. F., and P. M. Sprinkle. *The Faith of Jesus Christ: Exegetical, Biblical, and Theological Studies.* Peabody, MA: Hendrickson, 2009.
Black, D.A. *Scribes and Scriptures: Essays in Honor of J. Harold Greenlee.* Winona Lake, IN: Eisenbrauns, 1992.
Black, D. A., editor. *Rethinking New Testament Textual Criticism.* Grand Rapids: Baker Academic, 2002.
Bock, D. L. *Luke 1:1—9:50.* BECNT. Grand Rapids: Baker, 1994.
Bovon, F. *Luke 1: A Commentary on the Gospel of Luke 1:1—9:50.* Hermeneia. Minneapolis: Fortress, 2002.
Brown, R. E. *The Death of the Messiah: From Gethsemane to the Grave: A Commentary on the Passion Narratives in the Four Gospels.* New York: Doubleday, 1994.
Bruce, F. F. *Commentary on the Book of the Acts: The English Text, with Introduction, Exposition, and Notes.* The New International Commentary on the New Testament. Grand Rapids: Eerdmans, 1988.
———. *Commentary on the Epistle to the Hebrews.* The New London Commentary on the New Testament. London: Marshall, Morgan and Scott, 1964.
Büchsel, F., γενεά, κτλ, *TDNT* 1:662–65
Bultmann, Rudolf, εὐλαβής, κτλ, *TDNT* 2:751–54.

Burkitt, F. C. "On St. Mark XV: 34 in Cod. Bobiensis." *JTS* 1 (1900) 278–79.
Byrne, B. *Romans*. Sacra Pagina 6. Collegeville, MN: Liturgical, 1996.
Caird, G. B. "The Exegetical Method of the Epistle to the Hebrews." *CJT* 5 (1959) 44–51.
Campbell, D. A. "The Story of Jesus in Romans and Galatians." In *Narrative Dynamics in Paul: A Critical Assessment*, edited by B. W. Longenecker, 97–124. Louisville: Westminster: John Knox, 2002.
Carey, H. J. *Jesus' Cry from the Cross*, LNTS 398, New York: T. & T. Clark, 2009.
Childs, B. S. *Introduction to the Old Testament as Scripture*. Philadelphia: Fortress, 1979.
———. *Isaiah*. The Old Testament Library. Louisville: Westminster John Knox, 2001.
Clark, A. C. *The Primitive Text of the Gospels and Acts*. Oxford: Oxford University Press, 1914.
Clivaz, C. *L'Ange et la sueur de sang: Lc 22, 43–44*. Biblical Tools and Studies 7. Leuven: Peeters, 2010.
Collins, A. Y. *The Gospel According to Mark*. Hermeneia; Philadelphia: Fortress, 2007.
Colwell, E. C. *Studies in Methodology in Textual Criticism of the New Testament*. New Testament Tools and Studies 9. Leiden: Brill, 1969.
Comfort, P. W., and D. P. Barrett. *The Text of the Earliest New Testament Greek Manuscripts*. Wheaton: Tyndale, 2001.
Cranfield, C. E. B. *A Critical and Exegetical Commentary on the Epistle to the Romans*. 2 vols. ICC. Edinburgh: T. & T. Clark, 1982.
Davies, P., and B. Chilton, "The Aqedah: A revised Tradition History," *CBQ* 40 (1978) 514–46.
Dahl, N. A. "The Atonement—an Adequate Reward for the Akedah? (Ro 8:32)." In *Neotestamentica Et Semitica: Studies in Honour of Matthew Black*, edited by E. E. Ellis and M. E. Wilcox, 15–29. Edinburgh: T. & T. Clark, 1969.
Davis, E. F., and R. B. Hays. *The Art of Reading Scripture*. Grand Rapids: Eerdmans, 2003.
Dodd, C. H. *According to the Scriptures: The Sub-Structure of New Testament Theology*. London: Nisbet, 1952.
Edwards, J. R. *The Gospel According to Mark* The Pillar New Testament Commentary. Grand Rapids: Eerdmans, 2002.
———. "Markan Sandwiches: The Significance of Interpolations in Markan Narratives." *NovT* 31 (1989) 193–216.
Ehrman, B. D. *Lost Christianities: The Battle for Scripture and the Faiths We Never Knew*. New York: Oxford University Press, 2003.
———. *Misquoting Jesus: The Story of Who Changed the Bible and Why*. San Francisco: HarperSanFrancisco, 2005.
———. *The Orthodox Corruption of Scripture: The Effect of Early Christological Controversies on the Text of the New Testament*. New York: Oxford University Press, 1993.
———. "The Text as Window." In *The Text of the New Testament in Contemporary Research: Essays on the Status Quaestionis*, edited by B. D. Ehrman and M. W. Holmes, 361–79. Grand Rapids: Eerdmans, 1995.
Ehrman, B. D., and M. W. Holmes. *The Text of the New Testament in Contemporary Research: Essays on the Status Quaestionis*. Grand Rapids: Eerdmans, 1995.
Ehrman, B. D., and M. A. Plunkett. "The Angel and the Agony: The Textual Problem of Luke 22:43–44." *CBQ* 45 (1983) 401–16.
Ellens, J. H. *The Healing Power of Spirituality: How Faith Helps Humans Thrive*. 3 vols. Santa Barbara: Praeger, ABC-CLIO, 2010.

Ellingworth, P.. *The Epistle to the Hebrews: A Commentary on the Greek Text NIGTC*. Grand Rapids: Eerdmans, 1993.

Elliott, J. K. "The Case for Thoroughgoing Eclecticism." In *Rethinking New Testament Textual Criticism*, edited by D. A. Black, 101-24. Grand Rapids: Baker Academic, 2002.

———. *The Language and Style of the Gospel of Mark*. Supplements to *NovT* 71. Leiden: Brill, 1993.

———. "Review of J Harold Greenlee, *The Text of the New Testament: From Manuscript to Modern Edition*." *RBL* 1 (2009). Online: http://www.bookreviews.org/bookdetail.asp?TitleId=6605&CodePage=6605.

———. "When Jesus Was Apart from God: An Examination of Hebrews 2:9." *Expository Times* 83 (1972) 339-41.

Ellis, E. E. "How the New Testament Uses the Old," in *New Testament Interpretation: Essaus on Principles and Methods*, edited by I. Howard Marshall, 199-219. Exeter: Paternoster, 1977.

———. *Paul's Use of the Old Testament*. Edinburgh: Oliver and Boyd, 1957.

———. *Prophecy and Hermeneutic in Early Christianity: New Testament Essays*. Grand Rapids: Eerdmans, 1978.

Enns, P. *Exodus Retold: Ancient Exegesis of the Departure from Egypt in Wis 10:15-21 and 19:1-9*. Harvard Semitic Monographs 57. Atlanta: Scholars, 1997.

Epp, E. J. *Perspectives on New Testament Textual Criticism: Collected Essays, 1962-2004*. Supplements to *NovT* 116. Leiden: Brill, 2005.

———. *The Theological Tendency of Codex Bezae Cantabrigiensis in Acts*. SNTS Monograph Series 3. Cambridge: Cambridge University Press, 1966.

Evans, C. A. "Jewish Exegesis." In *DTIB*, 380-84.

Evans, C. A., and J. A. Sanders. *Luke and Scripture: The Function of Sacred Tradition in Luke-Acts*. Eugene, OR: Wipf & Stock, 2001.

Evans, C. A., and  E. Tov. *Exploring the Origins of the Bible*, Grand Rapids: Baker Academic, 2008.

Fee, G. D. *God's Empowering Presence: The Holy Spirit in the Letters of Paul*. Peabody, MA: Hendrickson, 1994.

———. *Paul's Letter to the Philippians*. The New International Commentary on the New Testament. Grand Rapids: Eerdmans, 1995.

———. "Textual-Exegetical Observations on 1 Corinthians 1:2, 2:1, and 2:10." In *Scribes and Scriptures: New Testament Essays in Honor of J. Harold Greenlee*, edited by D. A. Black, 1-15. Winona Lake, IN: Eisenbrauns, 1992.

Fishbane, M. *Biblical Interpretation in Ancient Israel*, Oxford: Oxford University Press, 1985.

Fitzmyer, J. A. *The Acts of the Apostles, A New Translation with Introduction and Commentary*. AB 31. New York: Doubleday, 1997.

———. *The Gospel According to Luke: Introduction, Translation, and Notes*. AB 28. Garden City: Doubleday, 1981.

———. *Romans: A New Translation with Introduction and Commentary*, AB 33. New York: Doubleday, 1993.

France, R. T. *The Gospel of Mark: A Commentary on the Greek Text*. NIGTC. Grand Rapids: Eerdmans, 2002.

Freedman, D. N., editor. *The Anchor Bible Dictionary*. 6 vols. New York: Doubleday, 1992.

Frei, H. W. *The Eclipse of Biblical Narrative: A Study in Eighteenth and Nineteenth Century Hermeneutics*. New Haven: Yale University Press, 1974.
Gamba, C. G. "Agonia Di Gesu." *RivB* 16 (1968) 159–66.
Green, J. B. *The Gospel of Luke*. New International Commentary on the New Testament 42. Grand Rapids: Eerdmans, 1997.
Greene, T. M. *The Light in Troy: Imitation and Discovery in Renaissance Poetry*. Elizabethan Club Series 7. New Haven: Yale University Press, 1982.
Greene-McCreight, K. *Feminist Reconstructions of Christian Doctrine: Narrative Analysis and Appraisal*. New York: Oxford University Press, 2000.
Grenfell, B. P., and A. S. Hunt. *The Oxyrhynchus Papyri 7*. Graeco-Roman Branch. London: Egypt Exploration Fund, 1910.
Grundmann, W. *Das Evangelium Nach Lukas*. Theologischer Handkommentar Zum Neuen Testament. Berlin: Evangelischer Verlagsantalt, 1966.
Gunkel, H. *Die Psalmen*. Vol. Abt. 2, Bd. 2. 4. Aufl. ed. Göttinger Handkommentar Zum Alten Testament. Göttingen: Vandenhoeck & Ruprecht, 1926.
Haines-Eitzen, K. *Guardians of Letters: Literacy, Power, and the Transmitters of Early Christian Literature*. New York: Oxford University Press, 2000.
Harnack, A. Von. "Probleme Im Texte Der Leidensgeschichte Jesu." *Studien zur Geschicte des Neuen Testaments und der alten Kirche* 1 (1931) 86–104.
Hawthorne, G. F., and R. P. Martin. *Philippians*. WBC 43. Nashville: Nelson, 2004.
Hays, R. B. *The Conversion of the Imagination: Paul as Interpreter of Israel's Scripture*. Grand Rapids: Eerdmans, 2005.
———. *Echoes of Scripture in the Letters of Paul*. New Haven: Yale University Press, 1989.
———. *The Faith of Jesus Christ: An Investigation of the Narrative Substructure of Galatians 3:1—4:11*. Dissertation Series, Society of Biblical Literature. Chico: Scholars, 1983.
———. *The Moral Vision of the New Testament*. San Francisco: Harper San Francisco, 1996.
Head, P. M. "Five New Testament Manuscripts: Recently Discovered Fragments in a Private Collection in Cambridge." *JTS* 59 (2008) 521–45.
———. "The Habits of New Testament Copyists: Singular Readings in the Early Fragmentary Papyri of John." *Biblica* 85 (2004) 299–408.
———. "Observations on Early Papyri of the Synoptic Gospels, Especially on the 'Scribal Habits.'" *Biblica* 71 (1990) 240–47.
Hollander, J. *The Figure of Echo: A Mode of Allusion in Milton and After*. Berkeley: University of California Press, 1981.
Holmes, M. W. "The Text of the Matthean Divorce Passages: A Comment on the Appeal to Harmonization in Textual Decisions." *JBL* 109:4 (1990) 651–64.
Hooker, M. D. *Jesus and the Servant: The Influence of the Servant Concept of Deutero-Isaiah in the New Testament*. London: SPCK, 1959.
Hort, F. J. A. *Two Dissertations*. London: Macmillan, 1876.
Hort, F. J. A. and Westcott, B. F. *The New Testament in the Original Greek*. 2 Vols. Cambridge: Cambridge University Press, 1882.
Housman, A. E. *Selected Prose*. Edited by J. Carter. Cambridge: Cambridge University Press, 1962.
Huck, A., and Greeven, H. *Synopsis of the First Three Gospels*. Tübingen: Mohr, 1981.
Instone-Brewer, D. *Techniques and Assumptions in Jewish Exegesis before 70 CE*. Tübingen: Mohr, 1992.

Irenaeus. *Against Heresies*. ANF 1. Grand Rapids: Eerdmans, 1979.
Janowski, B., and P. Stuhlmacher. *The Suffering Servant: Isaiah 53 in Jewish and Christian Sources*. Grand Rapids: Eerdmans, 2004.
Jellicoe, S. *The Septuagint and Modern Study*. Winona Lake, IN: Eisenbrauns, 1993.
Jeremias, J. *New Testament Theology: The Proclamation of Jesus*. New York: Scribner, 1971.
Käsemann, E. *Commentary on Romans*. Translated and edited by G. W. Bromily. Grand Rapids: Eerdmans, 1980.
Kee, H. C. "The Function of Scriptural Quotations and Allusions in Mark 11–16." In *Jesus Und Paulus: Festschrift für Werner Georg Kümmel Zum 70. Geburtstag*, edited by E. E. Ellis and E. Grasser, 165–85. Göttingen: Vandenhoeck & Ruprecht, 1975.
Kümmel, W. G. *Römer 7 und Die Bekehrung Des Paulus*. Untersuchungen Zum Neuen Testament, Heft 17. Leipzig: J. C. Hinrichsche, 1929.
Kidner, D. *Psalms 73–150: A Commentary on Books III–V of the Psalms*. Tyndale Old Testament Commentaries 14b. Downers Grove, IL: InterVarsity, 1973.
Kilpatrick, G. D. *A Greek–English Diglot for the Use of Translators: Luke*. London: British and Foreign Bible Society, 1962.
———. *The Principles and Practice of New Testament Textual Criticism: Collected Essays*. Edited by J. K. Elliott. Leuven: Leuven University Press, 1990.
Kittel, G., and G. Friedrich, *Theological Dictionary of the New Testament*. 10 Volumes. Translated by G. W. Bromily. Grand Rapids: Eerdmans, 1964–76.
Lake, K., F. J. Foakes-Jackson, and H. J. Cadbury. *The Beginnings of Christianity*. Vol. 4. London: Macmillan, 1920.
Lampe, G. W. H. "Grievous Wolves (Acts 20:29)." In *Christ and Spirit in the New Testament : Studies in Honour of Charles Francis Digby Moule*, edited by B. Lindars and S. S. Smalley, 253–68. Cambridge: Cambridge University Press, 1973.
Lane, W. L. *Hebrews 1–8*. WBC 47A. Dallas: Word, 1991.
Larkin, W. J. "The Old Testament Background of Luke xxii: 43–44." *NTS* 25 (1974) 250–54.
LeDauet, R. "Le Targum De Gen 22,8 Et 1 Pet 1,20." *RSR* 49 (1961) 103–6.
Levenson, J. D. *The Death and Resurrection of the Beloved Son: The Transformation of Child Sacrifice in Judaism and Christianity*. New Haven: Yale University Press, 1993.
Lightfoot, J. B. *Notes on the Epistles of Paul from Unpublished Commentaries*. London: Macmillan, 1895.
Lindars, B. *New Testament Apologetic: The Doctrinal Significance of the Old Testament Quotations*. London: SCM, 1961.
Longenecker, B. W. *Narrative Dynamics in Paul: A Critical Assessment*. Louisville: Westminster John Knox, 2002.
Lohmeyer, E. *Der Brief an Die Philipper*. 9 ed. Göttingen: Vandenhoech & Ruprecht, 1953.
Manson, T. W. "The Old Testament in the Teaching of Jesus." *BJRL* 34 (1951–1952) 312–32.
Marcus, J. *The Way of the Lord: Christological Exegesis of the Old Testament in the Gospel of Mark*. Louisville: Westminster John Knox, 1992.
Marshall, I. H. *New Testament Interpretation: Essays on Principles and Methods*. Exeter: Paternoster, 1977.
Mays, J. L. *Psalms*. Interpretation: A Bible Commentary for Teaching and Preaching. Louisville: Westminster John Knox, 1994.

Mbuvi, A. M. *Temple, Exile, and Identity in 1 Peter.* LNTS 345. London; New York: T. & T. Clark, 2007.

Metzger, B. M. *The Early Versions of the New Testament: Their Origin, Transmission, and Limitations.* Oxford: Oxford University Press, 1977.

———. *A Textual Commentary on the Greek New Testament.* 2nd ed. Stuttgart: Deutsche Biblegesellschaft; United Bible Societies, 1994.

Metzger, B. M., and B. D. Ehrman. *The Text of the New Testament: Its Transmission, Corruption, and Restoration.* 4th ed. New York: Oxford University Press, 2005.

Miller, M. "The Function of Isaiah 61:1-2 in 11Q Melchizidek." *JBL* 88 (1969) 467-69.

Minette de Tillesse, G. *Le Secret messiannique dans l'Evangile deMarc.* Paris: Cerf, 1968.

Moo, D. J. *The Old Testament in the Gospel Passion Narratives.* Sheffield: Almond, 1983.

Morris, L. "The Theme of Romans." In *Apostolic History and the Gospel: Biblical and Historical Essays Presented to F. F. Bruce,* edited by W. W. Gasque and R. P. Martin. 249-63. Grand Rapids: Eerdmans, 1970.

Moulton J. H., and G. Milligan. *The Vocabulary of the Greek New Testament: Illustrated from the Papyri and Other Non-Literary Sources.* 1930. Reprinted, Peabody, MA: Hendrickson, 1997.

Newman, C. C. *Jesus and the Restoration of Israel: A Critical Assessment of N. T. Wright's Jesus and the Victory of God.* Downers Grove, IL: InterVarsity, 1999.

Nolland, J. *Luke.* WBC 35B. Dallas: Word, 1993.

O'Brien, P. T. *The Epistle to the Philippians: A Commentary on the Greek Text.* NIGTC. Grand Rapids: Eerdmans, 1991.

Pao, D. W. *Acts and the Isaianic New Exodus.* Grand Rapids: Baker Academic, 2002.

Pao, D. W., and E. J.Schnabel. "Luke." In *Commentary on the New Testament Use of the Old Testament,* edited by G. K. Beale and D. A. Carson, 251-414. Grand Rapids: Baker Academic, 2007.

Parker, D. C. *An Introduction to the New Testament Manuscripts and Their Texts.* Cambridge: Cambridge University Press, 2008.

———. *The Living Text of the Gospels.* Cambridge: Cambridge University Press, 1997.

Parry, R. "Narrative Criticism." *DTIB,* 528-31.

Perrin, N. *Jesus the Temple,* Grand Rapids: Baker Academic, 2010.

Pietersma, A., and B. G. Wright, editors. *A New English Translation of the Septuagint and Other Greek Translations Traditionally Included Under That Title.* New York: Oxford: Oxford University Press, 2007.

Pitre, B. J. *Jesus, the Tribulation, and the End of the Exile.* Grand Rapids: Baker Academic, 2005.

Reicke, B."Jesus in Nazareth—Luke 4:14-30." In *Das Wort Und Die Worter: Festschrift G. Friedrich Zum 65: Geburtstag,* edited by H. Balz and S. Schulz, 47-55. Stuttgart: Kohlhammer, 1973.

Resseguie, J. L. *Narrative Criticism of the New Testament: An Introduction.* Grand Rapids: Baker Academic, 2005.

Rhoads, D. M., J. Dewey, and D. Michie. *Mark as Story: An Introduction to the Narrative of a Gospel.* 2nd ed. Philadelphia: Fortress, 1999.

Robinson, J. A. T. *Wrestling with Romans.* London: SCM, 1979.

Rodgers, P. R. "Luke 4:18: To Heal the Brokenhearted." In *The Healing Power of Spirituality: How Faith Helps Humans Thrive,* vol. 1, edited by J. H. Ellens, 163-69. Santa Barbara: Praeger, 2010.

---. "The New Eclecticism: An Essay in Appreciation of the Work of Professor George D. Kilpatrick." *NovT* 34 (1992) 388-97.
---. Review of *Guardians of Letters*, by Kim Haines-Eitzen, *NovT* 44 (2002) 404-7.
---. Review of *Misquoting Jesus* by Bart D. Ehrman. *The Christian Century* (July 11, 2006) 38-39.
---. "The Text of John 1:34." In *Theological Exegesis: Essays in Honor of Brevard S. Childs*, edited by C. R. Seitz and K. Greene-McCreight, 299-305. Grand Rapids: Eerdmans, 1999.
---. "Textual Criticism." *DTIB*, 784-87.
Royse, J. R. *Scribal Habits in Early Greek New Testament Papyri*. New Testament Tools, Studies and Documents 36. Leiden: Brill, 2007.
---. "Scribal Tendencies in the Transmission of the Text of the New Testament," In *The Text of the New Testament in Contemporary Research : Essays on the Status Quaestionis*, edited by B. D. Ehrman and M. W. Holmes, 239-52. Grand Rapids: Eerdmans, 1995.
Sanday, W., C. H. Turner, and A. Souter. *Novum Testamentum Sancti Irenaei*. Old-Latin Biblical Texts 7. Oxford: Clarendon, 1923.
Sanders, J. A. "From Isaiah 61 to Luke 4." In *Luke and Scripture*, edited by C. A. Evans and J. A. Sanders, 75-106. Eugene: Wipf & Stock, 2001. Originally in *Christianity, Judaism and Other Greco-Roman Cults: Studies for Morton Smith at Sixty*. Studies in Judaism in Late Antiquity 12, edited by J. Neusner. Leiden: Brill, 1975.
Schürmann, H. *Das Lukasevangelium*. Herders Theologischer Kommentar Zum Neuen Testament 58. Freiburg: Herder, 1969.
Segal, A. F. "'He Who Did Not Spare His Own Son . . .': Jesus, Paul and the Akedah." In *From Jesus to Paul: Studies in Honour of Francis Wright Beare*, edited by P. Richardson and J. C. Hurd, 169-84. Waterloo, ON: Wilfrid Laurier University Press, 1984.
Silva, M. *Philippians*. 2nd ed. BECNT. Grand Rapids: Baker Academic, 2005.
---. "The Text of Galatians: Evidence from the Earliest Greek Manuscripts." In *Scribes and Scripture: New Testament Essays in Honor of J.Harold Greenlee*, edited by D. A. Black, 17-26, Winona Lake, IN: Eisenbrauns, 1982.
Stec, D. M. *The Targum of Psalms*. The Aramaic Bible 16. Collegeville: Liturgical, 2004.
Stendahl, K. *Paul among Jews and Gentiles, and Other Essays*. Philadelphia: Fortress, 1976.
---. *The School of St. Mattew and Its Use of the Old Testament*. Acta Seminarii Neotestamentici Upsaliensis 20. Lund: Gleerup, 1954.
Stowers, S. K. *A Rereading of Romans: Justice, Jews, and Gentiles*. New Haven: Yale University Press, 1994.
Streeter, B. H. *The Four Gospels: A Study of Origins, Treating of the Manuscript Tradition, Sources, Authorship and Dates*. London: Macmillan, 1924.
Tasker, R.V.G. "Text of the 'Corpus Paulinum.'" *NTS* 1-2 (1954-55) 180-91.
Tischendorf, C. von. *Novum Testamentum: Editio Octava Critica Maior*. 2 vols. Lipsig: Hinrichs, 1872.
Tov, E. *Textual Criticism of the Hebrew Bible*. 2nd ed. Minneapolis: Fortress, 2001.
Turner, C. H. *The Gospel According to St. Mark*. London: SPCK, 1930.
Vanhoozer, K. J, C. G. Bartholoomew, D. J. Treier, and N. T. Wright, *Dictionary for Theological Interpretation of the Bible*, Grand Rapids: Baker Academic, 2005.
Vermes, G. *The Changing Face of Jesus*. New York: Penguin, 2002.

———. *The Dead Sea Scrolls in English*. London: Penguin, 2004.
———. *Jesus in His Jewish Context*. Minneapolis: Fortress, 2003.
———. *Scripture and Tradition in Judaism: Haggadic Studies,* Studia Post-Biblica 4. Leiden: Brill, 1961.
Volf, M. *Exclusion and Embrace: A Theological Exploration of Identity, Otherness, and Reconciliation*. Nashville: Abingdon, 1996.
Wagner, J. R. *Heralds of the Good News: Isaiah and Paul "In Concert" in the Letter to the Romans*. Supplements to *NovT* 101. Leiden: Brill, 2002.
Walls, A. F. *The Missionary Movement in Christian History: Studies in the Transmission of Faith*. Maryknoll: Orbis, 1996.
Watts, R. E. *Isaiah's New Exodus in Mark*: Biblical Studies Library. Grand Rapids: Baker, 2000.
Weber, R. *Le Psautier Romain Et Les Autres Psautiers Latins. Collectanea Biblica Latina 10*. Rome: Vatican Library, 1953.
Westcott, B. F. and F. J. A. Hort. *The New Testament in the Original Greek*. Vol. 2. London: Macmillan, 1882.
Williams, C. S. C. *Commentary on the Acts of the Apostles*. New York: Harper, 1957.
Wilson, J. P. "Romans viii 28: Text and Interpretation," *Expository Times* 60 (1948-49) 110-11.
Witherington III, B. *The Paul Quest: The Renewed Search for the Jew of Tarsus*. Downers Grove, IL: InterVarsity, 1998.
Wright, C. J. H. *The Mission of God: Unlocking the Bible's Grand Narrative*. Downers Grove, IL: InterVarsity, 2006.
———. "The Year of Jubilee." *ABD* 5 (1982) 1025-30.
Wright, N. T. *The Challenge of Jesus: Rediscovering Who Jesus Was and Is*. Downers Grove, IL: InterVarsity, 1999.
———. *Jesus and the Victory of God*. Christian Origins and the Question of God 2. Minneapolis: Fortress, 1996.
———. *Justification: God's Plan & Paul's Vision*. Downers Grove, IL: InterVarsity, 2009.
———. *The New Testament and the People of God*. Christian Origins and the Question of God 1. Minneapolis: Fortress, 1992.
———. *The Resurrection of the Son of God*. Christian Origins and the Question of God 3. Minneapolis: Fortress, 2003.
Wordsworth, J., W. Sanday, and H. J.White, *Old Latin Biblical Texts, No. II*. Oxford: Clarendon, 1886.
Yoder, J. H. *The Politics of Jesus: Vicit Agnus Noster*. Grand Rapids: Eerdmans, 1972.
Zuntz, G. *The Text of the Epistles: A Disquisition upon the* Corpus Paulinum. Schweich Lectures, 1946. London: British Academy, 1953.

# Index of Names

Aland, B., 50, 73, 103
Aland, K., 50, 73, 103
Alter, R., 52
Attridge, H. W., 33, 41–42

Bailey, K. E., 96
Balch, D., 98
Barrett, C. K., 17, 78
Barrett, D. P., 73, 86
Bauckham, R., 29, 59
Beale, G. K., 10
Bellinger, W. H., 57
Bengel, J. A., 36
Bird, M. F., 11
Black, D. A., 18
Bock, D. A., 54, 98
Bolte, K., 15
Bovon, F., 96–98
Brown, R. E., 55–56
Bruce, F. F., 33, 64, 69
Büchsel, F., 90
Bultmann, R., 40
Burkitt, F. C., 45–46
Byrne, B., 78

Cadbury, H. J., 69
Caird, G. B., 36
Campbell, D. A., 66
Carey, H. J., 48
Carson, D. A., 10
Childs, B. S., 60, 80
Chilton, B., 66
Clark, A. C., 73, 85–86
Clivaz, C., 54
Collins, A. Y., 84
Colwell, E. C., 3

Comfort, P. W., 73, 86
Cranfield, C. E. B., 17–19

Dahl, N. A., 27
Davies, P., 66
Dewey, J., 4, 87
Dodd, C. H., 9, 11–12, 18, 25, 34–36, 48, 69, 105

Edwards, J. R., 48, 87–88, 91
Ehrman, B. D., 6–10, 22–24, 31–34, 44–47, 49, 55–58, 60, 62–63, 85–86, 95, 101–2, 105
Ellens, J. H., 16, 93
Ellingworth, P., 34
Elliott, J. K., 15, 34, 55, 85, 87
Ellis, E. E., 9, 12, 28
Enns, P., 13
Epp, E. J., 5–6, 9–10, 105
Evans, C. A., 91, 97–98

Farmer, W. R., 57
Fee, G. D., 2, 73, 77
Fishbane, M., 13, 89, 90
Fitzmyer, J. A., 17–18, 23–24, 27, 54–55, 64–65, 70, 77–78, 82, 94, 98
France, R. T., 84–85
Frei, H. W., 11, 71

Gamba, C. G., 56
Green, J. B., 26, 96
Greene-McCreight, K., 11, 15
Greene, T. M., 35
Greenlee, H., 85
Greeven, H., 54

117

Gregory, J., 15
Grundmann, W., 94
Gunkel, H., 48
Guthrie, G. H., 36

Haines-Eitzen, K., 24, 57–58, 60, 73–74
Harnack, A. von, 40, 45, 47
Hawthorne, G. F., 5
Hays, R. B., 9, 11–14, 20, 29, 35–40, 48–49, 59, 98, 105
Head, P. M., 3, 77, 96
Headlam, A. C., 17
Hollander, J., 38
Holmes, M. W., 3, 95, 104
Hooker, M. D., 57
Hort, F. J. A., 2, 17, 55, 56, 64, 78
Housman, A. E., 1
Huck, A. 54
Hunt, A. S., 72

Instone-Brewer, D., 16

Janowski, B., 57
Jellico, S., 81
Jeremias, J., 25

Käsemann, E., 17
Kee, H. C., 50–51
Kidner, D., 67
Kilpatrick, G. D., 15, 18, 54
Kümmel, W. G., 83

Lake, K., 69
Lampe, G. W. H., 68
Lane, W. L., 32, 36, 42
Larkin, W. J., 57
LeDauet, R., 27
Levenson, J. D., 15, 67
Lightfoot, J. B., 69
Liid, D., 15
Lindars, B., 9, 51, 52
Lohmeyer, E., 72
Longenecker, B. W., 11

Manson, T. W., 47
Marcus, J., 36, 48–49, 51, 59
Marshall, I. H., 28
Martin, R. P., 5
Mays, J. L., 67
Mbuvi, A. M., 13
McCain, S., 15–16
Metzger, B. M., 2–4, 22–23, 31–32, 46, 62, 64, 78, 85–86, 94–95, 102
Michie, D., 4, 87
Miller, M., 97
Minette de Tillesse, G., 88
Moo, D. J., 48
Morris, L., 18
Moulton, J. H., 96

Newman, C. C., 13
Nolland, J., 56

O'Brien, P. T., 73

Pao, D. W., 13, 57–59
Parker, D. C., 6, 8–10, 56, 104–5
Parry, R., 4
Perrin, N., 51
Pietersma, A., 39, 82
Pitre, B. J., 91
Plunkett, M. A., 55

Reicke, B., 96–97
Resseguie, J. L., 4
Rhoads, D. M., 4, 87
Robinson, J. A. T., 18
Rodgers, P. R., 2, 16, 23–25, 58, 60, 106
Royse, J. R., 3, 102

Sanday, W., 17, 46, 94
Sanders, J. A., 97, 99
Schnabel, E. J., 57–58
Schürmann, H., 94
Segal, A. F., 65
Silva, M., 19, 72

Spinks, C., 16
Sprinkle, P. M., 11
Stec, D. M., 82
Stendahl, K., 9, 11–12, 47, 83
Stowers, S. K., 78–79
Streeter, B. H., 60
Stuhlmacher, P., 57

Tasker, R. V. G., 33
Tischendorf, C. von, 33, 54, 76, 95
Tov, E., 10, 91, 102–3
Turner, C. H., 27, 45, 47, 94

Vermes, G., 15, 27, 64–66, 97
Vinson, D. R., 15
Volf, M., 100

Wagner, J. R., 13, 36, 59, 82

Walls, A. F., 103
Walters, J., 36
Watts, R. E., 13, 59
Weber, R., 81
Westcott, B. F., 17, 55–56, 64
White, H. J., 46
Williams, C. S. C., 63
Wilson, J. P., 18
Witherington III, B., 12
Wordsworth, J., 46
Wright, C. J. H., 14, 99
Wright, N. T., 12–13, 15–16, 75, 88, 91, 97

Yoder, J. H., 99

Zuntz, G., 32

# Index of Scripture and Ancient Sources

## OLD TESTAMENT

**Genesis**

| | |
|---|---|
| 3:19 | 57 |
| 22 | 27–30, 64–65, 67–68, 70 |
| 22:1 | 49, 51 |
| 22:2 | 25, 27, 65 |
| 22:12 | 25, 27, 51 |
| 22:16 | 25, 27, 51 |
| 37–50 | 15 |
| 50:20 | 19–20, 104 |

**Leviticus**

| | |
|---|---|
| 25 | 97 |
| 25:10 | 99 |
| 26 | 90 |
| 26:34–35 | 90 |

**Deuteronomy**

| | |
|---|---|
| 21:23 | 49 |
| 32 | 91 |
| 32:5 | 90–91 |
| 32:20 | 91 |

**Joshua**

| | |
|---|---|
| 2:10 | 51 |

**1 Kings**

| | |
|---|---|
| 19:5–6 | 57 |

**2 Kings**

| | |
|---|---|
| 15–17 | 91 |
| 24–25 | 91 |

**2 Chronicles**

| | |
|---|---|
| 3:1 | 65 |
| 36:18–21 | 90 |
| 36:19–21 | 90 |

**Job**

| | |
|---|---|
| 42:2 | 57 |

**Psalms**

| | |
|---|---|
| 2 | 29, 36 |
| 2:7 | 22, 24–27, 29, 49, 51, 104 |
| 8 | 36, 41–42 |
| 8:4–6 | 36, 40–41 |
| 8:5–7 | 33 |
| 8:6 | 33 |
| 8:7 | 42 |
| 11:6–7 | 57 |
| 18:49 | 37 |
| 21 (LXX) | 34, 38, 47 |
| 21:1 (LXX) | 49 |
| 21:25 (LXX) | 39 |
| 22 | 34–40, 42, 47–49, 51–53, 58, 60, 80, 103, 105 |
| 22:1–21 | 38 |
| 22:1 (22:2 MT; 21:2 LXX) | 34–35, 37–38, 42, 44, 48–49, 53, 104 |
| 22:2 | 34, 57 |
| 22:3 | 57 |
| 22:7 | 48 |
| 22:15 | 57 |
| 22:18 | 48, 58 |

**Psalms** (*cont.*)

| | |
|---|---|
| 22:22–31 | 38 |
| 22:22 | 34, 37–40, 42 |
| 22:25 | 40 |
| 30 | 80 |
| 31:5 | 37 |
| 32 | 83 |
| 32:1–2 | 82 |
| 35 | 48 |
| 38 | 48 |
| 40 | 37 |
| 41 | 48 |
| 51 | 83 |
| 68 (LXX) | 49, 51 |
| 69 | 47–49, 51–53, 80, 103 |
| 69:1–22 | 51 |
| 69:9 | 37 |
| 69:10 | 48 |
| 69:21 | 48 |
| 69:23–29 | 51–52 |
| 69:25 | 48 |
| 69:26 | 52 |
| 69:30–36 | 51 |
| 69:35 | 51 |
| 73:2 (LXX) | 67–68 |
| 73:8 (LXX) | 69 |
| 73:18 (LXX) | 69 |
| 74 | 67–70 |
| 74:1–11 | 67 |
| 74:2 | 67–68 |
| 74:9 | 69 |
| 74:12–17 | 67 |
| 74:18–23 | 67 |
| 89:9 | 57 |
| 95:7–11 | 36 |
| 110 | 36, 49 |
| 110:1–4 | 36 |
| 110:1 | 42, 51 |
| 110:4 | 25 |
| 118:22–23 | 51 |
| 118:25–26 | 51 |
| 129 (LXX) | 82 |
| 129:1 (LXX) | 82 |
| 129:3 (LXX) | 82 |
| 129:8 (LXX) | 82 |
| 130 | 80–83, 105 |
| 130:1–3 | 80 |
| 130:3 | 82 |
| 130:4 | 80–81 |
| 130:5–6 | 80 |
| 130:7–8 | 81 |
| 130:8 | 82 |
| 142:2 | 35 |
| 143 | 12, 83 |
| 143:2 | 12, 35 |

**Proverbs**

| | |
|---|---|
| 3:11–12 | 36 |

**Isaiah**

| | |
|---|---|
| 5:1–2 | 51 |
| 8:16–18 | 39 |
| 8:17–18 | 37 |
| 25–26 | 75 |
| 26 | 74, 76 |
| 26:3 | 74–75 |
| 26:19 | 76 |
| 34:4 | 51 |
| 40–55 | 26, 36 |
| 40 | 50 |
| 40:3–5 | 60 |
| 40:3 | 50–51 |
| 42 | 29 |
| 42:1–4 | 26 |
| 42:1–2 | 25 |
| 42:1 | 25–27, 49, 51 |
| 43 | 69–70 |
| 43:21 | 69–71 |
| 51–55 | 59 |
| 51:17 | 57 |
| 51:22 | 57 |
| 53 | 5, 49, 57–58, 60 |
| 53:3 | 57, 60 |
| 53:8 | 87 |
| 53:11 | 50 |
| 53:12 | 57–58, 60 |
| 56:7 | 51 |
| 58:6 | 93, 96, 98 |

## Index of Scripture and Ancient Sources 123

**Isaiah** (*cont.*)
| | |
|---|---|
| 61 | 93–94, 96–97, 99 |
| 61:1–2 | 60, 96–98 |
| 61:1 | 94, 96, 99 |
| 61:1c | 97 |

**Jeremiah**
| | |
|---|---|
| 7:11 | 51 |
| 25 | 89–90 |
| 25:9–12 | 90 |
| 25:15 | 57 |
| 25:17 | 57 |
| 25:28 | 57 |
| 31:31–34 | 36, 50 |

**Ezekiel**
| | |
|---|---|
| 23:31–34 | 57 |
| 32:7–8 | 51 |

**Daniel**
| | |
|---|---|
| 3:28 | 57 |
| 7 | 49 |
| 7:13–14 | 51 |
| 7:13 | 51 |
| 9 | 88–90 |
| 9:3 | 88, 92, 105 |
| 9:32 | 89 |

**Habakuk**
| | |
|---|---|
| 1:1—2:4 | 36 |
| 2:3–4 | 36 |
| 2:4 | 35 |

**Zechariah**
| | |
|---|---|
| 8:19 | 88 |
| 9:9 | 51 |
| 9:11 | 50 |
| 12:2 | 57 |

**Malachi**
| | |
|---|---|
| 3:1 | 50–51 |

**Jubilees**
| | |
|---|---|
| 17:15 | 65 |
| 18:3 | 65 |

**4 Maccabees**
| | |
|---|---|
| 6:29 | 66 |
| 13:12 | 66 |
| 16:20 | 66 |
| 17:21–22 | 66 |
| 18:18–19 | 91 |

~

## NEW TESTAMENT

**Matthew**
| | |
|---|---|
| 3:16 | 107 |
| 3:17 | 22, 25 |
| 5:32 | 104 |
| 6:10–12 | 86 |
| 6:33 | 107 |
| 7:14 | 107 |
| 7:18 | 107 |
| 8:9 | 107 |
| 8:21 | 107 |
| 12:18 | 26 |
| 15:14 | 107 |
| 15:31 | 107 |
| 16:21 | 107 |
| 17:21 | 86, 92, 104 |
| 20:30 | 107 |
| 23:26 | 107 |
| 26:39 | 55 |
| 27:16 | 107 |
| 27:17 | 107 |
| 27:46 | 38, 44, 47, 53, 104 |

**Mark**
| | |
|---|---|
| 1:1 | 4 |
| 1:2–3 | 51 |
| 1:11 | 22, 25, 51, 104 |
| 1:41 | 45 |
| 2 | 87, 89 |
| 2:1–3 | 50 |
| 2:18–22 | 87 |
| 2:18 | 89 |

## Mark (cont.)

| | |
|---|---|
| 4 | 13 |
| 4:20 | 107 |
| 8:27–30 | 89 |
| 9:12 | 88 |
| 9:14–29 | 88, 90 |
| 9:19 | 90 |
| 9:29 | 16, 84–90, 92, 101–2, 104–5 |
| 9:30–32 | 88 |
| 9:30 | 85 |
| 9:32 | 89 |
| 10:45 | 49, 58 |
| 11:1–11 | 51 |
| 12:1–12 | 51 |
| 12:23 | 107 |
| 13:24–26 | 51 |
| 14:62 | 49, 51, 58 |
| 14:72 | 107 |
| 15 | 48–49 |
| 15:23 | 48 |
| 15:24 | 48 |
| 15:29 | 48 |
| 15:34 | 7, 38, 44–49, 51, 53, 101, 103–5 |
| 15:36 | 48 |

## Luke

| | |
|---|---|
| 2:25 | 88 |
| 3:22 | 7, 22–26, 29, 95, 101, 104 |
| 3:44–46 | 60 |
| 4 | 94, 97–99 |
| 4:16–30 | 93, 97–98, 100 |
| 4:18 | 16, 92–102, 104 |
| 4:21 | 60, 99 |
| 6:27–28 | 99 |
| 9:31 | 29, 60 |
| 11:14 | 107 |
| 22:37 | 57, 59–60 |
| 22:43–44 | 8, 53–61, 101–2, 104 |
| 23:34 | 58, 100 |
| 23:34a | 58 |
| 23:34b | 59 |
| 23:46 | 37 |
| 24:44 | 28 |

## John

| | |
|---|---|
| 1:18 | 2 |
| 1:34 | 22, 25 |
| 1:49 | 26 |
| 2:17 | 37, 48 |
| 7:53—8:11 | 2 |
| 13:2 | 107 |
| 13:32 | 107 |
| 16:13 | 107 |
| 19:28 | 37 |

## Acts

| | |
|---|---|
| 1:20 | 48 |
| 13:32–33 | 25 |
| 10:30 | 85 |
| 20 | 67–69 |
| 20:18–35 | 64 |
| 20:28 | 8, 27, 62–71, 101, 103–5 |
| 20:29 | 68–69 |

## Romans

| | |
|---|---|
| 1:17 | 35 |
| 1:28 | 19 |
| 3 | 12, 35 |
| 3:20 | 12, 35 |
| 4 | 4 |
| 4:1 | 14 |
| 4:7 | 82 |
| 5:1 | 2, 23, 107 |
| 6:19 | 82 |
| 7–11 | 80–83 |
| 7–8 | 80 |
| 7 | 78–79, 82–83 |
| 7:7—11:36 | 82 |
| 7:7—8:4 | 79 |
| 7:7–25 | 79 |
| 7:7–24 | 82 |
| 7:21 | 80 |
| 7:24–25 | 79 |
| 7:24 | 80, 82 |

## Romans (cont.)

| | |
|---|---|
| 7:25 | 80, 107 |
| 8:2 | 77–92, 104–5 |
| 8:15 | 81 |
| 8:23–25 | 81 |
| 8:28 | 15, 17–21, 101–2, 104–5 |
| 8:32 | 27, 65 |
| 8:39 | 82 |
| 9–11 | 20, 59, 81–82, 105 |
| 11:32 | 82 |
| 11:33 | 82 |
| 15 | 58–59 |
| 15:3 | 37, 48 |

## 1 Corinthians

| | |
|---|---|
| 2:1 | 2 |
| 5:13 | 107 |
| 7:5 | 85 |
| 11:23–25 | 50 |
| 15 | 33 |
| 15:27b | 33 |

## Galatians

| | |
|---|---|
| 3–4 | 4 |
| 3:13 | 49, 53 |
| 4:21—5:1 | 28 |

## Philippians

| | |
|---|---|
| 1:20 | 75 |
| 2:6–8 | 5 |
| 2:10 | 74 |
| 2:25 | 74 |
| 3 | 72, 83 |
| 3:2 | 74 |
| 3:14 | 73 |
| 3:21 | 107 |
| 4 | 72 |
| 4:7 | 72–76, 101–2, 104 |
| 4:18 | 74 |

## Colossians

| | |
|---|---|
| 1:7 | 107 |
| 4:14 | 96 |

## Hebrews

| | |
|---|---|
| 1–8 | 32, 42 |
| 1:5 | 25 |
| 2 | 33, 39–40, 42, 103 |
| 2:6–8 | 40–41 |
| 2:6 | 33 |
| 2:9 | 31–44, 101–2, 104–5 |
| 2:10–12 | 37 |
| 2:12 | 34, 36, 38–40, 42 |
| 5:5–6 | 25 |
| 5:7 | 35–36, 38, 40 |
| 5:12 | 107 |
| 10:5–7 | 37 |
| 11:17–19 | 27 |

## James

| | |
|---|---|
| 3:3 | 107 |
| 4:14 | 107 |

## 1 Peter

| | |
|---|---|
| 1:20 | 27 |
| 2 | 58 |
| 2:23 | 52 |
| 3:15 | 104 |

## 1 John

| | |
|---|---|
| 5:18 | 107 |

## Revelation

| | |
|---|---|
| 9:13 | 107 |
| 15:6 | 107 |
| 18:3 | 107 |
| 18:8 | 107 |
| 19:6 | 107 |
| 19:7 | 107 |
| 19:11 | 107 |
| 21:4 | 107 |

## ANCIENT SOURCES

### Dead Sea Scrolls

| | |
|---|---|
| 4Q225 | 65, 70 |
| 11QMelch | 97, 99 |

### Euripides
*Medea*

| | |
|---|---|
| 1077–1080 | 79 |

### Irenaeus
*Against Heresies*

| | |
|---|---|
| 3.11.7 | 44 |
| 4.8.1 | 94 |

### Jerome
*Epistles*

| | |
|---|---|
| 106 | 81 |

### Josephus
*Antiquities*

| | |
|---|---|
| 1.222–236 | 66 |

### Justin
*Dialogue with Trypho*

| | |
|---|---|
| 88 | 22, 30 |
| 103 | 30 |

### Liber Antiquitatem Biblicarum

| | |
|---|---|
| 18:5 | 66 |
| 32:2–4 | 66 |
| 40:2 | 66 |

### Origen
*Contra Celsum*

| | |
|---|---|
| 2.24 | 56 |

*de Oratione*

| | |
|---|---|
| 39.19 | 19 |

## MANUSCRIPTS DISCUSSED

| | |
|---|---|
| $P^{16}$ | 72–73 |
| $P^{72}$ | 74 |
| ℵ (01) | 54–55, 73, 85 |
| B | 73, 85 |
| D | 23, 45 |
| 0311 | 77–78 |
| 1739 | 32 |
| k | 46 |

www.ingramcontent.com/pod-product-compliance
Lightning Source LLC
Chambersburg PA
CBHW072156160426
43197CB00012B/2410